BRINGING TIME TO LIFE

This book is being translated into other languages.
For availability, please contact
The Professional Development Institute.

A.P. MARTIN

BRINGING TIME TO LIFE

120 practical tips
for managing your time
and enjoying life

 The Professional Development Institute

Cambridge, Massachusetts and Ottawa, Ontario

U.S. Library of Congress Catalog Card Number: 94-67886

Canadian Cataloguing in Publication Data

Martin, A.P. (Alain Paul)
   Bringing time to life : 120 practical tips for
managing your time and enjoying life

Includes bibliographical references and index.
ISBN 0-86502-023-X

   1. Time management.   2. Self-actualization
   (Psychology) I. Professional Development Institute.
   II. Title

HD69.T54M37   1994   650.1   C94-900631-9

   The Professional Development Institute PDI Inc.
   79 Fentiman Avenue, Ottawa, ON K1S 0T7 Canada
   Tel: (613) 730-7777 or (819) 772–7777   Fax: (613) 235-1115

Graphics: Maurice Sabourin
Jacket design: M. Sabourin, T. Sécheresse (RTA Advertising, Montréal)
Production: Rick Martinelli
Publication: Janet Elias
Publisher: The Professional Development Institute PDI Inc.
Printer: PDI Press
Printed in Canada

This book is dedicated to the volunteers
of The Red Cross, UNICEF
and Médecins sans frontières
who make time for us.

Foreword

Our personal time is a precious gift. A scarce and non-renewable resource, it should be invested no less wisely than other valuable assets. This book is an invitation to self-examination and self-discipline which are necessary to nurture our total growth — physical, emotional, professional or spiritual. It is about the quality of time we share with those we love and care for. And it is about making and saving time to fulfill our mission and to take up gratifying challenges both at work and at home.

Perhaps, most important, it is about taking the time to enjoy life.

Saving time sounds like simple common sense. If so, why all the books offering advice on the subject? And why am I writing yet another book?

Our experience at the Harvard Planner Group has amply demonstrated that the subject of time management is anything but simple. And certainly not common. Too many people equate time management with efficiency and a race against the clock: doing it faster must be doing it better. Nothing could work more adversely against an effective performance. Nor is the race against time limited to the inexperienced, as one might expect. Ironically, as we scan the corporate ladder, we note an increasing degree of stress and burnout the closer we get to the top.

In her recent research at The Harvard Business School, Juliet Schor found no evidence linking long working hours with higher productivity.[1] On the contrary, constant overwork has two inherent risks. It gives rise to flawed decisions and, all-too-often, to illness.

During the last twenty-five years, I have served a dozen large companies from Boeing, Du Pont and General Electric to Skanska Cement (Stockholm), Boliden of Sweden and CAP Gemini of Great Britain and The Netherlands. I have seen too many executives retire in poor health or die in the job. In my ten-year consulting practice with Desjardins, a highly successful corporation with $75 billion in assets, I have observed a staggering death toll in the executive suite. Many senior executives, including a Chief Executive Officer, were either forced to leave before retirement for health reasons or have passed away while at work. Heart failures from stress and overwork top the list of predicaments.

These disturbing events have gradually consolidated my interest in time management. While Desjardins is now well on its way to becoming a world-class leader in both business and occupational health, the majority of corporations still ignore the plight they are in.

Further experience with the Asian Productivity Organization in Hong Kong and the Engineering Advancement Association of Japan, gave me an additional impetus to my ongoing research in this field. In Japan, job-related back pain, eye ailments and *Karoshi* – death by overwork – are endemic.

Yet, everywhere clients consistently acknowledge the fact that they have no shortage of ideas about what to do with their time, if only they could find the time to work on these ideas. A considerable work backlog is omnipresent in most decision-makers' minds and offices.

In order to alleviate that backlog and help people work effectively, our practical research has led to the creation of proven time-management instruments and products.

Through the use of a systematic approach to time management developed in our consulting practice and seminars, we have been able to help clients strike a delicate balance between economy, efficiency and effectiveness. Moreover, we have demonstrated that equity, ethics and equilibrium (the other triple E) can be fully integrated into daily action plans even as we maintain our corporate stability and personal well-being.

Clients come to us distressed by the sense that although they are working harder than ever, important jobs are being left undone or rushed to the finished line.

Clients leave us confident that their new know-how and skills in time management can eliminate the dysfunctional stress and frustration of too much on their plates. Instead of counting minutes, they make minutes count.

Among our products, the Harvard Planner®2 brings tangible benefits at an affordable cost to decision-makers, professionals and students throughout the world. Our clients are saving millions of corporate dollars and improving their own health by applying the principles of Proactive Thinking and by using the Harvard Planner®, the Global Method® and the Global Software.

Because stress and time-wasting are omnipresent in our society, we want to share our unique life-planning concepts with a wider audience of aspiring leaders, professionals and students.

But make no mistake: time management is not a quick fix. It is neither perfectionism nor an end in itself. Even the best time management behavior will not bring instant gratification. As a means to a better quality of life, time management aims at doing a superior job *the first time* with less stress and less paperwork. However, the road to success is mined with obstacles and failures. But failure is a valuable form of feedback which can lead to success.[3] What characterizes winners more than anything else is that they don't quit when they face failure. Learning what is involved in making our performance more effective is only the first and smallest step. Putting the know-how into practice over the long haul is the only way to excellence. As Blair Bergstrom, an editor of The Harvard Business Review and an eloquent critic of the one-minute management fix, has written:

> I think we're being insulted. The professional practice of management is as challenging and complex as the practices of medicine and law. Yet, we never hear of a one-minute brain surgeon or a one-minute trial lawyer. One minute is about how long the physician or attorney who tries it will last.
>
> The quick fix. The too simple solution. The latest fad. They have no more place in your office than

in the operating room or the courtroom. Excellence in any profession cannot be achieved overnight. You learn the basics in school. You sharpen your skills in the practice of your profession. And if you mean to excel, you keep up with new thoughts and ideas by reading a professional journal.[4]

Thus, beware of cookbook recipes; the struggle to lead a fulfilling life never ends. Practice and ongoing learning are imperative to convert principles and tips into skills.

We have grouped the suggestions and tips for taking control of your time into 12 sections:

1. Get the facts first; take time to think
2. Plan wisely; be mission-driven
3. Concentrate on priorities; leverage your time
4. Reduce your total workload; increase your effectiveness
5. Think teamwork, delegate, seek help
6. Organize your space; use the best time savers
7. Cut down on paperwork; value productive technology
8. Subject the phone to the bottom line
9. Run productive meetings
10. Travel carefree
11. Stretch your body and soul
12. Make life worth living

Under these sections, each suggestion or tip starts with a short sentence in boldface. If the subject is not relevant to you, your team or your family, skip to the next point. If pertinent, read further. Does the suggestion trigger ideas that would help you save time and live better?

As you read this book[5], write down your thoughts in the space for personal notes. Share the content with your work team, family and friends. Helping them to harness the power of time to improve their performance at work and to achieve more of their life goals with less stress is the most valuable gift you can give.

References and notes

1. Juliet Schor, *The Overworked American,* Basic Books, Harper Collins, New York, 1991, ISBN 0-465-05434-X, $12.

2   *The Harvard Planner®* is a genuine timesaving invention with U.S. and foreign patents, created by the author. An independent evaluation performed by Ernst & Young and the patents issued in the USA, Canada and Japan confirm the fact that the Planner is a genuine saver of both time and space. A registered trademark of Harvard University, The Harvard Planner® is available in several models, sizes and languages, book bound, *Wire-O* bound or in 3-, 6- or 7-hole refills from The Harvard Planner Group at (819) 772-7777, Fax: (613) 235-1115. Prices vary from $5 to $31.

3. Bobbi Deporter & Mike Hernacki, *Quantum Learning – Unleashing the Genius in You,* Dell Publishing, DoubleDay, New York, NY, 1992, page 95, ISBN 0-440-50427-9.

4. A. Blair Bergstrom, *The One-minute What?* Letter about the Harvard Business Review, March 30, 1990.

5. Some important sentences are repeated under the pertinent tips to facilitate selective readings or reinforce the concepts. Regarding the references, several excerpts were selected from the upcoming book *The Proactive*

Thinking Paradigm which goes beyond the topic of time management. This is particularly the case for the sections on setting missions and priorities. Thus, the reader does not have to wait for my next book to gain detailed insights into these crucial topics. Having these excerpts, you are therefore not required to get *The Proactive Thinking Paradigm* unless you have a vested interest in the fields of scanning, issue incubation, stakeholders' analysis and strategy formulation.

Acknowledgment

I am particularly indebted to Hélène Martin, Anne Scholten, Raymonde Lavoie, Tina Schiefelbein and Janet Elias for their professional advice and practical suggestions to refine the structure, the style and content of this book. My deepest gratitude goes to Hanh Do Doan, Marie-Pascale Parmentier and Maurice Sabourin for their invaluable support in the strenuous task of deciphering my notes and proofreading the endless drafts of the 50 original tips which now number 120 on the last count! Many thanks also to Susan Bruneau and to PDI Press Director, Rick Martinelli and his dedicated staff Paul Leduc, Hélène Pharand, Marc Sabourin, Dean Whittington, and to the RTA creative staff for completing the cover under inelastic production deadlines. I wish to acknowledge the following authors and publications quoted in *Bringing Time to Life*:

Back Basics, Back Association of Canada, Toronto, Ontario;

Melodie Beattie, *Codependent No More*, Hazelden Educational Materials, Center City;

Herbert Benson; *Time out from Tension,* Harvard Business Review, 1978;

A. Blair Bergstrom, *The One-Minute What?* Harvard Business Review, 1990;

Allan Bloom, *The Closing of the American Mind,* Simon and Schuster, New York, 1987;

Réflections d'Alphonse Desjardins, La Confédération des caisses populaires et d'économie Desjardins du Québec, Lévis, Québec;

Mihaly Csikszentmihalyi, *The Evolving Self,* Harper Collins Publishers, 1993;

Mihaly Csikszentmihalyi, *Flow: The Psychology of Optimal Experience, Steps Toward Enhancing the Quality of Life,* Harper Perennial, 1990;

Edward de Bono, *de Bono's Thinking Course,* Facts on File, New York, 1985;

General Electric, *Work-Out,* GE Croton-on-Hudson, NY;

Maxwell Maltz, *Creative Living for Today,* Simon & Schuster, 1974;

Aaron Mattes, *Flexibility-Active and Assisted Stretching,* Aaron Mattes Publishers, Sarasota, Florida;

Hugh Prather, *Notes to Myself, My struggle to become a person,* Bantam Books, New York, 1976;

Juliet Schor, *The Overworked American,* Harper Collins Publishers, New York, 1991; and

Susan Silver, *Organized to be Best,* Adams-Hall Publishing, Los Angeles, CA.

Many thanks to my clients including Boeing, Bombardier, GE, and particularly John Harbour of the Desjardins Confederation and his remarkable team of executives who orchestrate a world-class financial conglomerate, and who spared no effort to validate and implement these timesaving tips throughout their organization. I wish also to thank Prof. John Sviokla of The Harvard Business School for encouraging me to pursue my research on timesaving. His encouragement prompted the impetus for the writing of this book. Finally, I alone am responsible for the book content, errors and omissions.

A.P. Martin

Table of Contents

Foreword. ix

Acknowledgment. xvii

SECTION 1

Get the facts first. Take time to think.

1. Take time to think. 1
2. Question your own perceptions
    and knowledge. 4
3. Be informed. 4
4. Probe assumptions, claims, and
    news headlines. 5
5. Know where your time goes. 5
6. Audit your work every year. 5
7. Phase out time-wasters. .8
8. Do not compromise on ethics. 10

SECTION 2

Plan wisely. Be mission-driven.

9. Set worthwhile goals/objectives. 19
10. Above all, be mission-driven. 24

11. Validate each objective.................... 30
12. Display the essential goals and targets....... 30

SECTION 3

Concentrate on Priorities.
   Leverage your time the Proactive way.

13. Determine priority before urgency............35
14. Define urgency without falling into
     its traps.................................39
15. Schedule and prune your workload
     constantly................................ 42
16. Formulate viable strategies................. 43
17. Manage risk............................... 43
18. Break objectives into small tasks
     and milestones............................ 44
19. State targets to measure what matters........ 44
20. Set specific time for scheduling
     every day................................. 44
21. Prepare daily *do-lists* with the
     Harvard Planner®......................... 44
22. Avoid perfectionism on routine
     obligations............................... 45
23. Be flexible...............................46

SECTION 4

Reduce your workload.
   Increase your effectiveness.

24. Invest your prime time in what
     you value most........................... 51

25. Give your total attention to one topic at a time.............................51
26. Avoid anarchy and constant interruptions................................52
27. Don't be a jack-of-all-trades.................52
28. Learn to say *no* even to your best friends..................................52
29. Commute wisely...........................53
30. Reduce your workload by making lasting decisions............................53
31. Value pre-programmed decisions............55

SECTION 5

Think teamwork. Delegate & seek help.

32. Understand the driving forces of your workload.............................63
33. Don't delegate what you can eliminate...................................64
34. Consider the skill level......................65
35. Delegate gradually by apprenticeship.........66
36. Provide excellent support..................68
37. Monitor results..........................68
38. Discuss the specific shortcomings............68
39. Reward fairly and praise generously..........68
40. Stay lean. Build lasting alliances.............69
41. Invest in your ultimate freedom..............69
42. Question your behavior....................69

SECTION 6

Organize your space. Use the best time savers.

43. Arrange your working area.................73
44. Don't compromise on stationery............ 74
45. Shop for the best time savers.............. 74
46. Think prevention and
    unconditional warranties.................. 75
47. Integrate time into all your
    buying decisions.......................... 75
48. Plan and cluster your purchases.............76
49. Don't clutter your desk.................... 76
50. Think security............................ 77
51. Back up your Harvard Planner®
    and valuable documents....................78

SECTION 7

Cut down on paperwork.
Value productive technology.

52. Avoid the incoming mail and fax traps....... 83
53. Handle each document only once............ 84
54. Dictate or write letter outlines only..........84
55. Avoid buzzwords...........................85
56. Learn to type. It is never too late........... 85
57. Speed up tracking your plans
    and work.................................. 86
58. Move away from ad-hoc activities........... 86
59. Help your readers save time................. 86
60. Create documents that provoke
    a lasting impression....................... 87
61. Automate cautiously.......................87

62. Run computers and software wisely.......... 88
63. Value productive technology................88

SECTION 8

Subject the phone to the bottom line.

64. Take advantage of smart phones
    and cellular technology.................... 93
65. Schedule and consolidate your calls.......... 95
66. Reduce time spent looking for
    phone numbers............................ 95
67. Don't invite trivial work.................... 96
68. Handle incoming calls skillfully............. 96
69. Be polite and brief......................... 97
70. Log your incoming messages................ 97
71. Work in pairs.............................. 98

SECTION 9

Run productive meetings.

72. Question the need and frequency
    of meetings...............................103
73. Know your audience.......................103
74. Use the *Meeting Form* of
    The Harvard Planner®.................... 104
75. Plan meetings carefully.................... 104
76. Select the best date and location
    for the participants........................ 105
77. Choose visuals that promptly get
    your message across....................... 105
78. Simulate alternative scenarios.............. 105

79. Rehearse................................. 106
80. Avoid the last minute rush............... 106
81. Start meetings on time................... 106
82. Start with important issues.............. 107
83. Value the power of silence............... 107
84. Stay on course. Orchestrate a
     genuine dialogue......................... 107
85. Inspire goodwill......................... 108
86. Refrain from responding to
     personal attacks......................... 108
87. Record decisions......................... 108
88. Show appreciation and celebrate.......... 109

SECTION 10

Travel carefree.

89. Assess the cost/benefits of travel....... 113
90. Save money and time on personal
     and business trips....................... 113
91. Travel light............................. 116
92. Plan a safe and comfortable trip........ 118
93. Avoid overnight transatlantic flights.... 120
94. Beware of the trap of the new
     taxicab driver........................... 120
95. Save time on travel reports.............. 121
96. Sleep well............................... 121
97. Don't give up exercise................... 121
98. Plan your meals.......................... 121
99. Manage your wake-up time................. 122

SECTION 11

Stretch your body and soul.

100. Prevent stress risks and burnouts...........127
101. Remain alert..............................128
102. Curtail night-shift work and driving......... 128
103. Watch your diet and liquor consumption.....129
104. Recharge your batteries.................... 130
105. Prevent sleeping disorders................. 130
106. Treasure and protect your
     moments of solitude...................... 131
107. Exercise................................. 131
108. Reward yourself.......................... 134

SECTION 12

Make life worth living.

109. Cherish genuine friendships............... 141
110. Socialize tactfully........................ 141
111. Build allies.............................. 142
112. Have fun.................................142
113. Don't poison your life.................... 142
114. Don't slip into codependency status......... 143
115. End dysfunctional relationships gracefully.... 143
116. Stop reading and watching trivia........... 143
117. Concentrate on the vital few...............144
118. Prune work backlog at least once a month... 144
119. Learn new skills to face greater
     challenges every day...................... 144
120. Take time off............................145
121. Break the *work-and-spend* vicious cycle...... 145

122. Be altruistic at least once a day............146
123. Experience flow.........................146
124. Record your achievements.................147
125. Seize the day, the moment................ 147

30-day Action Plan.........................**155**
Index......................................**161**

About the Author

Section 1

Get the facts first

Take time to think

1. Take time to think.

On important issues, even when the solution seems obvious, take time to think or at least pause before rushing to implement a decision. When you reach a major conclusion or finish a proposal, if feasible, try to hold it for at least one night just in case you discover a flaw or a better idea.

It may sound paradoxical to suggest that *thinking slowly* would improve your performance in time management. Yet, we all know about assignments where imposed or self-inflicted time pressure led to more problems than solutions. In brain-intensive tasks, speed is a frequent impediment. Edward de Bono warns against this time trap in his *Thinking Course* which was instrumental to my performance as an inventor, a writer and a decision-maker. He states:

> Most of the time we think far too quickly. I include myself in that *'we'*. Perhaps tests and examinations have persuaded us that there is a value in getting to the answer as quickly as

possible. Yet, from a thinking point of view that
is wrong. Even in an emergency, there is plenty
of time to think slowly. In hotel fires most
deaths are caused by panic. Instead of zooming
through to a conclusion we need to think
slowly—step by step . . . We confuse quick
understanding with quick thinking . . . The
simple habit of trying to think more slowly can
make a big difference to our effectiveness as
thinkers . . . Thinking slowly means we can
focus more clearly on each stage. There are also
specific focusing tools we can use. [1]

Alas, most decision-makers escape to action. They find
deep uninterrupted thinking intolerable.

In 1974, I was asked to direct an emergency food
assistance program to rescue thousands of flood victims
abroad. In order to generate viable options, I invited
the team members to think quietly for five minutes
before making suggestions. An executive shouted
angrily: "Why go through the agony of thinking when
the solution is obvious? All we need is plain action now:
airlifting food from Canada."

As a compromise, I asked him to spend five minutes
considering all factors related to his idea while everyone else searched for a better way. Within this short
timeframe, someone suggested that rather than
airlifting food from Canada we should ask the Food
and Agricultural Organization (FAO) to put its field
experience to work for us and take care of the delivery.
The idea was accepted by everyone including the
executive! So, while en route for another assignment

in the Middle-East, I stopped in Rome overnight to contract with the FAO to buy sorghum and high-protein grains from neighboring countries to reach the victims promptly. Within 48 hours, our assistance was reaching the recipients. Meanwhile, the major donor nations, who opted for airlifting food, were still struggling with the logistics. The only highway between the airport and the flooded area was washed away by torrential rains. The FAO knew better. It used ground transportation on the dry side of the river.

Since then, I have witnessed projects ranging from nuclear power plants to telecommunication and software systems where the client paid a high price for implementing a solution that was rushed through design, engineering and other creative tasks. Creative work is brain-intensive. It is essential for risk identification and risk learning. Implementation work assumes that risks are already known. It deals with risk management as opposed to risk learning. Expediting brain-intensive tasks is frequently riskier than fast-tracking implementation. Fast thinking stresses the designers and triggers flaws that are not immediately apparent. It should be done only with great caution and as a last resort. Furthermore, the practice of accelerating critical activities to meet a tight schedule is widespread. Yet, there are better ways.[2]

As Alphonse Desjardins, the founder of the first great cooperative movement in North America, once said:

> We must stand on guard against the dangerous ambition to sacrifice the solid progress sought for immediate results . . . this does not call for

undue delays. Far from it, this thought is simply
an invitation to think, not to rush and later to
be forced to retreat, or to redo a job that was
performed in haste.[3]

Taking time to think, however, does not mean open
deadlines. That would be unrealistic. A time discipline
is necessary as we shall see in the section about priority-
setting.

2. Question your own perceptions and knowledge.

The increasing complexity of our world must humble
even the most talented and experienced experts among
us. Our limited knowledge is increasingly perishable.
The pressure for time can easily introduce biases in our
perceptions and skew our judgment toward a flawed
decision, which can affect our well-being and perhaps
the lives of others. The frame of reference we use to
see the world may be inaccurate or outdated. Questioning our knowledge, values, belief system and perceptions is an act of great wisdom.

Welcome feedback and resist the impulse to shoot the
messenger. Invest time in self-examination and in the
search for truth.

3. Be informed.

Scan for emerging opportunities and issues early.
Secure the information before it becomes available
through regular means. Learn how issues incubate.[4]

Daily news is highly perishable. Reading complete stories is time-consuming and subject to the law of diminishing returns, particularly for scientists and engineers who spend endless hours on literature search. Save time by reading only the top paragraph of news items and the last paragraph of editorials. If the content is pertinent, read further and concentrate to get the most out of it. If not, skip to the next story.

Use automated scanners and electronic information banks to speed up your search. Gradually build up your own electronic index of search keys.

4. Probe assumptions, claims and news headlines.

Challenge basic assumptions.[5] Beware of overstatements. Take sales claims and news headlines with a grain of salt. Strategic information from business and governments is carefully formulated and disseminated with economic and geopolitical interests in mind, even in democratic societies. Full disclosure is rare. So, validate the data and, when in doubt, seek credible references, before making important decisions.

5. Know where your time goes.

Question the value of each action you undertake. Always ask yourself why and why you? At least once a week, reconsider the relevance of unfinished actions.

6. Audit your work every year.

Lasting control over your time is wishful thinking

unless it is based on facts. The first step toward greater performance is to collect data about your behavior.

Each year, select seven days at random and log work, errands, interruptions and everything you do on a time log. For this purpose, a large variety of inexpensive forms is available commercially. However, many are simplistic in design and offer little if any guidance in analyzing time-wasters and in taking corrective action. The *Harvard Time Log*[6] is a unique and versatile instrument that permits you to quickly collect data and to analyze where your time goes and to draw immediate timesaving conclusions based on 16 practical questions including two of your own selection. Its purpose is quality auditing in the context of Total Quality Management (TQM).

Use your time log to study the time, duration and priority of each action in it. At the end of each of the seven randomly selected days, try to answer the following questions. Add your own questions.

– Did this action advance your business or personal objectives?
– Was it ethical? Was it good for your health, the community or the people you care about?
– Did it help your current or future career?
– Did it help the mission of your current or potential allies?
– Was it adequately planned?
– Were you the appropriate person to do it?
– Did you get adequate support from your team, management, peers or your family?

- Did you have the right tools and documentation?
- Were you sufficiently trained? Did you have the right skills?
- Were you given the required authority?
- Did you start/finish on or ahead of time?
- Did you deliver a high quality job or service?
- Was your work appreciated?
- Did you enjoy it?

Just asking these questions may lead you to some timesaving opportunities. At the very least, you are now on your way to identifying the sources of your time management problems.

Your time log should help you study recurrent time-wasters, explore solutions and prepare a game plan for change. These time-wasters include:

- insufficient time to think or to plan work adequately; unreasonable deadlines or time projections
- plans, objectives or data not systematically validated; fuzzy or biased work specifications
- unnecessary work or activities that neither add value to your mission nor are compulsory
- insufficient or unreliable support, poor delegation; clients, suppliers or managers not available when required
- unclear documentation; defective or inadequate tools, noisy or *unergonomic*[7] work stations
- non-pertinent reading materials, memos, unsolicited mail
- excessive time spent looking for people; walking

between offices, waiting on the phone or elsewhere, filing or searching computerized or hard-cover files
- cluttered desks and files; questionable record-keeping or redundant paperwork; poorly designed forms
- roles, responsibility and accountability either not clearly established or poorly communicated
- risk either underestimated or not explicitly assessed
- late deliveries
- unjustified perfectionism; lenient quality definition or control
- unproductive meetings and phone calls; interruptions; drop-in visitors
- inability to handle people who are troubled, disruptive or difficult
- travel, either excessive or inadequately planned
- ineffective use of daily commute time
- prolonged watching of trivia on TV or listening to banalities on radio or elsewhere
- unplanned or frequent shopping particularly on weekends
- procrastination and indecision

7. Phase out time-wasters.

Wasting time is like commiting suicide by installments.[8] Your time-wasters are revealed by negative answers to the 16 questions of the time log.

Internal or self-inflicted time-wasters such as procrastination and indecision are quietly robbing managers of hundreds of hours a year. Even external time-wasters such as incoming calls, drop-in visitors and meetings which may seem beyond your control can, within reason, be brought under your sphere of influence.

If the solution is obvious, go for it, particularly on routine issues. If not, be careful. The action may be an isolated event due to chance and may not occur again. Before investing in a costly or risky solution, ask the acid-test questions: Is this action recurrent or part of a pattern? How much of it is necessary?

Start by eliminating unnecessary work and wasted time in each activity in your job or in the *value chain* of your project. Then, re-engineer or improve actions that add value. Consider pre-programmed decisions, cautious automation, task combination, change of quality standards, change of task sequence, substitution with a quicker service, process simplification, reduction of the frequency of delivery or reduction of the amount of detail. It may also be faster to have the task performed outside of, or elsewhere in, your organization.

If time-wasting is due to difficult people, consider a seminar to gain skills on the topic or view the 26-minute video cassette *Working with Difficult People*. It is a lifetime investment well-worth the effort.[9]

Consider these tips merely as a source of thought. Innovate. Practice Edward de Bono's vertical and lateral thinking to produce creative and practical solutions.[10] Do not compromise quality. Success requires ongoing determination, tact, discretion and clever strategies. There are no quick fixes. Track your performance as indicated in the log. Showing progress is energizing in itself.

8. Do not compromise on ethics.

Question your own claims and behavior. Are they motivated by high standards of business ethics? Do you have
a clear and precise code of conduct?[11] Are your
decisions not only economically and strategically
sound, but also ethical?

The absence of a profound conviction of the need for
ethical leadership and for a proactive commitment to
enhance and preserve it by every manager and professional, is a fundamental cause of the most devastating
time-wasters in our society. Think of the social cost of
negligence, insider trading, antagonism, selfishness, tax
evasion, narcotics, speeding and other behaviors that
collectively rob us of precious time and the cost of
frequently letting time cheaters grow in our organizations.

As an illustration, many of us create bottlenecks by
remaining in the passing lane of divided highways, or
worse, we try to save fifteen minutes by exceeding the
speed limit. In the process we endanger life, pollute
more and risk losing far more time and money if we
have an accident or collect a traffic ticket. Also, think
of the time lost behind the wheel every day by thousands of commuters as a result of accidents due to
speeding, stress, incompetent or careless driving. In my
ten-year consulting practice with the casualty insurance
industry, I repeatedly noticed that tragic situations were
rarely motivated by mischief. The irresponsible behavior of the culprits was nearly always due to naiveté,
ignorance or complacency.

More individual accountability for wasting collective time is long overdue. Our freedom stops when it starts wasting the time of others.

I am frequently asked, "What is the point of bringing ethics into time management?" With the above, I hope we can now see the broader picture, namely that time-wasting is an omnipresent and growing predicament in our society.

Before blaming others, we must first get rid of our own perceptions, mental blocks and blind spots. And before calling for more government intervention, we must invest our own time in promoting and practicing integrity, honesty, fairness, active cooperation, public service and individual responsibility. Without bringing about these enduring values to our neighborhood and day-to-day behavior, our society risks working uphill forever.

References and notes

1. Edward de Bono, *de Bono's Thinking Course,* Facts
    on File, 40 Park Avenue South, New York, NY 10016,
    1985, ISBN 0-8160-1895-2.

2. A.P. Martin, *World Seminar: The Complete Project
    Management Cycle,* The Professional Development
    Institute, March 1994; available to all seminar
    participants.

3. *Réflexions d'Alphonse Desjardins*, edited by La
    Confédération des caisses populaires et d'économie
    Desjardins du Québec, 100, avenue des Commandeurs,
    Lévis, Québec, G6V 7N5 418-835-4403.

4. A.P. Martin, *The Proactive Thinking Paradigm,*
    Chapter I: Issue Incubation, The Professional
    Development Institute, 1995.

5. For insights on how we can postulate assumptions to
    explain industrial phenomena, read Eliahu M. Goldratt
    and Jeff Cox, *The Goal, A process for ongoing
    improvement,* North River Press, Box 309, Croton-on-
    Hudson, NY 10520, 1992 edition, ISBN 0-88427-061-0,
    $19.95.

6. *The Harvard Time Log* is available from The Harvard
    Planner Group. Tel: (819) 772-7777 or Fax: (613)
    235-1115, $10 for a two-year supply.

7. "Ergonomics is the science of making the work environment compatible with people so they can work more comfortably and productively. Ergonomics looks at the dimensions of work tables, desks and chairs and matches them to the wide range of body sizes and shapes.... When you pay close attention to these standards you can avoid such symptoms as fatigue, eyestrain, blurred vision, headaches, stiff muscles, irritability and loss of feelings in fingers and wrists." Excerpts from *Organized To Be Best!* by Susan Silver, Adams-Hall Publishing, Box 491002, Los Angeles, CA 90049 Tel: (310) 826-1851 or 1-800-888-4452.

8. Raymond Hull, *How to Get what You Want,* Simon & Schuster, Pocket Edition, Markham, Ontario, Canada, 1976, ISBN 0-671-78327-0.

9. The video cassette by Jack E. White, Larry Levy and Brian Weiss, *Working with Difficult People* is available from McGraw-Hill Training Systems.

    PDI and other training institutions offer in-house and public seminars on dealing with difficult people.

10. Recommended readings in creativity include:

    James L. Adams, *Conceptual Blockbusting: A Guide to Better Ideas,* W.H. Freeman and Company, 660 Market Street, San Francisco, CA 94104, 1974, ISBN 0-7167-0757-8.

Edward de Bono, *Lateral Thinking: Creativity Step by Step,* Perennial Library, Harper and Row, New York, 1973 edition, ISBN 0-06-090325-2, $12.

Edward de Bono, *Future Positive,* Penguin Books, 1979, ISBN 0-14-013778-5, $9.

Edward de Bono, *I am Right, You are Wrong: From This to The New Renaissance; From Rock Logic to Water Logic,* Foreword by three Nobel Prize winners, Penguin Books, 1991, ISBN 0-14-012678-3. $10.

Recommended viewing: *Edward de Bono's Thinking Course,* BBC Television Series, London, 1985. The book accompanying the videofilm is also available separately under the same title and is published by Facts on File, New York, 1985, Tel:(212) 683-2244, ISBN 0-8160-1892-2.

11.   For current research on business ethics, consult:

Thomas R. Piper, Mary C. Gentile and Sharon Daloz Parks, *Can Ethics Be Taught? Perspectives, Challenges, and Approaches at Harvard Business School,* Harvard Business School, Boston, MA, 1993, ISBN 0-87584-400-6, $19.95.

Kenneth R. Andrews, ed. *Ethics in Practice: Managing the Moral Corporation,* Harvard Business School Press, Boston, 1989.

Joseph L. Badaracco, Jr., and Richard R. Ellsworth: *Leadership and the Quest for Integrity,* Harvard Business School Press, Boston, 1989.

Caroline Whitebeck, *The Trouble with Dilemmas: Rethinking Applied Ethics,* Spring-Summer 1992.

Louis Racine, Georges A. Legault, Luc Bégin, *Éthique et Ingénierie,* McGraw-Hill, Montréal, 1991, ISBN 0-07-551296-3.

Fernando Savater, *Etica Para Amador,* Editorial Ariel, Barcelona, 1994; French version, *Éthique à l'usage de mon fils,* Editions du Seuil, 1994.

Personal notes

_____

_____

_____

_____

_____

_____

_____

_____

_____

_____

_____

_____

_____

_____

_____

_____

_____

_____

_____

_____

_____

_____

_____

Section 2

Plan wisely

Be mission-driven

9. Set worthwhile goals/objectives.

Setting achievable personal goals (or objectives) is one of the most difficult and important tasks of time management. A worthwhile goal implemented with a clever strategy brings fulfillment. A poor or invalid objective impedes our progress and may even hamper our future.

The pre-requisites for goal-setting are a clear mission; sound values and a deep awareness of our feelings, capabilities and potential for growth. Sometimes we need the inspiration and experience of others to set personal goals that stretch us to our full potential. Sometimes, the goals beyond our wildest dreams could be within our reach, if only we knew how to make the stretch.

Thanks to Herbert Shepard, I became aware of my potential as a lecturer and business speaker. He also provided me with the know-how and the environment to overcome my fears of speaking in public. M.I.T. professor Richard Beckhard encouraged me to write down my ideas about proactive thinking. Both mentors were invaluable in opening my eyes to goals I had never considered before. My career path was enriched beyond the Management Science consulting practice I had originally targeted for myself.

You too can seek the help of your mentor, parents, spouse, former professors, respected boss, admired friends, a counselor or a personal assessment center. They can help you identify your potential and gain further awareness about available opportunities, both personal and professional.

In addition, there are many practical publications on the topic of goal setting, including *Essence of a Proactive Life.*[1]

Unless written down, your goals will remain elusive and may even be forgotten. Before writing your personal goals, consider the following questions merely as a prelude for the exercise:

a) What do you value in life? Make an effort to identify the principles, qualities and personal policies that are most important to you — the values that govern your behavior and attitudes. Keep them in mind throughout the exercise.

b) What do you like? In order to answer this question:

- List the most inspiring persons in your life, the people you like as well as those you care about the most.

- List the 15 things you like to do most in life. If 15 sounds like too many, don't be discouraged. The first answers that come to mind may not be the most relevant after all. Many people discovered that the things they really liked were not obvious until they took the time to think and search for them.
- List your 15 major accomplishments.
- List the 15 best events that positively marked your life.

c) What do you do?

- List your past, current and emerging roles and functions, whether they are related to your job, family, community or other affiliations.
- List the 15 things you frequently did over the last 6 months, whether you liked them or not.
- List the people you met frequently over the last six months. What values and interests do you have in common? Are your differences a source of learning and gratification?
- List the 15 events and failures that negatively affected your life.
- What issues and challenges are you facing? How important are they to your present and future?
- What impediments do you still face? What are your obsessions and dependencies? Are they real or self-inflicted? What is not working well for you?

d) Summarize both the positive and negative feed-back you are getting about your behavior, attitudes, feelings, knowledge, skills and values from others, whether they are friends or foes, bosses or subordinates, colleagues or personal contacts.

e) What needs for change come to mind about your knowledge, skills, behavior, attitudes, feelings and values? What misconceptions or dysfunctional habits do you wish to undo?

f) What other aspirations, wishes or desires do you have now and in the past?

g) What are you good at? What are your proven talents and potential abilities? What would you like to learn if you ever had a chance?

h) What objectives/goals do you wish to achieve for your organization, family and community? Which of these goals are coherent with the principles and values you identified at the beginning of this exercise? Review the principles once more. Add important goals that were neglected so far but which would help you live by the values that govern your life. What changes would each goal require?

i) Whose support can you count on? At what cost (emotional, financial, other)?

Add more questions to systematically scan your world, your dreams, feelings, thoughts and aspirations.

Use answers to the above questions to draft a list of goals. Identify the benefits of each goal. As an illustration, assume you listed your daughter among the people you love, and tennis among the things you like. You may wish to consider playing tennis more frequently with your daughter as a goal, assuming she agrees. If you are concerned about your manager's feedback with respect to your writing skills, you should consider a seminar on the topic as a worthwhile goal.

By writing down the answers to the above questions, you are less likely to forget important goals that do not spontaneously come to mind. At this stage, do not restrict the number of goals; paper is cheap. In addition, you require a good base to choose from. The objective is to select the goals that have the greatest impact on your mission this year by ranking them, using priority and urgency. Note that mission, objective validity, priority and urgency are the subjects of the timesaving tips below.

Goals not selected for this year will either be postponed to future years or will be superseded by overriding needs.

You should review your life goals and values at least once a year. Draft your personal plan based on your values, aspirations and the corporate plan. Update the yearly plan once a month. Detail it once a week.

Take time to carefully plan important goals. These normally take a long time to reach. Anticipate obstacles. Don't give up at the first sign of failure. Constancy of purpose is vital to success.

10. Above all, be mission-driven.

Mission is a difficult and important topic covered in detail in *The Proactive Thinking Paradigm,*[2] from which the following notes were selected. After reading these notes, write or review your mission and highlight the above goals that add value to it.

Mission is the core reason for everything you do and the first commandment in any business establishment. A mission is the constitution, the bond or "the gluon"[3] that unites a group of people. It is the corporate signature that clearly differentiates between organizations even when they operate in the same field.

Individuals, no less than organizations, have a mission. However, for most people, the mission remains implicit until they face a surprise event. We are, unfortunately, a society driven by surprise events. In order to set a mission explicitly, one should ask the frightening question:

What do I want to do with my life at least in the foreseeable future?

This self-examination should preferably precede a surprise event when we are clear-headed.

Personal missions are our individual interpretations of what is meant by being a good person. They range from the fundamental notion of *"staying alive"* or *"charting a life worth living"* to *"donating our talent and abilities to make the world a better place for people and*

other beings. " Athletes may opt for *"stretching body
and soul to draw on their full potential. "* A visionary
may wish to work on *"achieving a new world order
for peace and prosperity. "* A working mission for a
management trainer can vary from *"developing and
coaching aspiring leaders"* to the broader goal of
*"helping professionals and managers improve their
performance at work. "* As we can see, the notion of
being a good person permeates each of these missions.

For a family, the mission is what keeps its members
together, what prevents them from leaving each other.
It is a manifestation of the value system, the beliefs
and the common cause to which the active members
ought to contribute. As Allan Bloom says, we should
keep in mind that "a value is only a value if it is life-
preserving and life-enhancing . . . Values are the core
of life . . . They have a necessity, a substantiality more
compelling than health or wealth . . . Authentic values
are those by which a life can be lived . . . Commitment values the values and makes them valuable."[4]

For an organization, the real mission is the product of
the dominant coalition, i.e. the small number of
powerful people who can, but rarely do, veto anything
the organization does. The dominant coalition is similar
to the critical mass[5], except that the critical mass is
issue-centered, while the influence of the dominant
coalition transcends issues. Identifying the dominant
coalition is the first task of decision-makers. The search
should not be restricted to staff or board members.
There are frequent instances in business and governments where the dominant coalition is made up of one
person namely a banker, a vendor, a customer, the

owner's spouse or mentor, a friend, an ambassador, the Secretary of State or the Chief of Defence Staff of a neighboring country. As a head of Systems Development of a large conglomerate in the early seventies, I quickly learned that the dominant coalition of the Systems Department was the Vice-President of a mainframe vendor who, fortunately, was skilled, prudent and honest, and for these reasons a valuable ally.

You should neither rush to formulate a strategy, nor set priorities before identifying the extent of overlap between your perception of the goals necessary to fulfill the mission and the perception of your dominant coalition. The larger the congruence of perceptions the better. Here are your five options:

- Ignore the goals that carry no adverse consequences if not done, and that at best, would add a marginal value to you, your allies and to the community at large.

- Consider a *wait and see* intervention or extreme caution for goals you value but which are alien to the coalition's view. Also explore this stance for goals of an uncertain value that require a feasibility study or a pilot experiment.

- Consider a *compliance* (i.e. doing the minimum to get by) or a *symptomatic intervention* for goals that are valued by the coalition but not shared by you.

- Consider an *active intervention* to do precisely what is expected, neither more nor less. This option is reserved for goals where there is no merit in exceeding the standards, the norm, the policy requirements or the quotas. Since the investment in time or resources to exceed the quotas will only yield marginal benefits, it should be spared for goals of greater value. Most decision-makers and professionals usually see the active option as the only choice, thus overlooking the other options. While an active stance may indeed be the only feasible alternative, we ought to explore the full range of avenues for each goal. When doing what is expected may not be enough to consolidate your competitive edge, think of the next option.

• Consider *proactive interventions* for goals of high value and which you share with the coalition. A proactive intervention aims at maximizing opportunity by doing better or more with less. Keep in mind that trying to be proactive everywhere is counterproductive.

If you are a newcomer to your organization, such prudent behavior permits you to build trust during your *honeymoon period* and to consolidate your power before embarking on the mission you value. Unfortunately, this is rarely the case. In managers' eagerness to appear as democratic and participative, newcomers are frequently at the mercy of the outspoken, rather than the wise or powerful stakeholders. You risk your reputation and career by rushing to implement a mission strongly biased by the view held by the most radical champions. By doing your homework, you may discover after a while that the coalition's perception of the mission is even more realistic than your own original view.

Most academics who write on this topic naively fail to stress the importance of the dominant coalition in the process of mission-setting. Linking the corporate mission to the dominant coalition is an inescapable reality which has important implications in strategic planning.

Within a company, a hierarchy of missions exists. Each unit of the organization ought to define its own mission clearly and review it on an ongoing basis, seriously taking into account the perception of the unit's dominant coalition. This practice inevitably sparks the question:

Should the mission of each unit be subordinated to that of its corporation?

This question is two-sided. On the one hand, the organization's units do not have to be totally subservient to the corporate mission. Indeed, the growth of an organization sometimes results from the initiative of constituents expanding their boundaries beyond the corporate turf. On the other hand, the survival of each unit may hinge on the extent to which its mission overlaps that of the parent organization.

For this reason, the mission of a company unit or a division should reflect a predominant contribution to its corporate "raison d'être." Otherwise, a dispersion of energy in endless directions occurs, thus endangering the corporation's existence.

Unlike objectives which have a finite life-cycle, a mission is neither finite nor infinite but *indeterminate in time-span.* Normally, no one knows in advance how long a mission will last.

Missions tend to be challenged following the occurrence of a surprise event. To avoid confusion, the corporate mission should, whenever feasible, be clearly communicated to each management tier before, rather than after, a surprise event. Whether you are in a position of power to change the mission or not, a mission-setting or review exercise should be performed at least once a year. Otherwise, your organization tends to grow in fruitless directions. Such pathological growth can lead to an identity crisis. The effect of the review is analogous to the constant pruning and weeding of an orchard to enable the trees to give better and more abundant yields. Its purpose is to clarify perceptions and make assumptions explicit. Otherwise, each manager would be working from an implicit, untested perception of the actual mission. This is not uncommon among corporate leaders, particularly when the published mission was formulated for public consumption.

Furthermore, overextending the mission beyond a manageable horizon often results in diffused and uncontrollable bureaucracies. Such temptation can be a trap for the unwary. It should, therefore, be eschewed in favor of contrivable territory to permit sound control, stability and adequate growth. For the dominant coalition to agree on these considerations, powerful and enlightened leaders are required at the helm. For more on mission, consult Chapter III of *The Proactive Thinking Paradigm.* [6]

In summary, there is no point in saving time without a clear constancy of purpose. Beyond the mission, all our efforts should be motivated by life-enhancing and life-preserving ethical values.

11. Validate each objective.

A valid objective or goal is expressed in real or potential benefits. It adds value to your mission, unless adopted by necessity for compliance. It is specific, ethical, realistic, reasonable, measurable and timebound. It does not destabilize the future of your family or organization by hoarding scarce resources. If you work in a team or have a spouse, you should share and validate your common goals to ensure synergy.

According to Nobel Prize winner Linus Pauling, good scientists are able to recognize and discard bad ideas and invalid objectives to avoid wasting time on flawed endeavors.[7] However, most of us tend to overlook the validity tests and to risk facing the adverse consequences of working on flawed goals/objectives. For detailed guidelines on how to validate complex objectives, refer to Chapter IV of *The Proactive Thinking Paradigm*.[8]

12. Display the essential goals and targets.

Visible boards are a constant reminder and a compelling force for action. With current technology, it is now possible to use large graphic displays at an affordable cost.

References and notes

1. Herbert A. Shepard, *Essence of a Proactive Life, 2 Practical Essays on Life and Career Planning,* The Professional Development Institute, 1994, $9.00.

2. A.P. Martin, *The Proactive Thinking Paradigm,* Chapter III "Mission-setting and Review: The First Commandment of Business", The Professional Development Institute, 1995, Tel: (819) 772-7777.

3. Gluon: a word borrowed from physics (quantum chronodynamics) and coined by Physicist Gell-Mann in referring to the invisible glue in the form of particles (quantas) that act as strong forces between quarks. The gluon keeps these particles together.

4. Allan Bloom, *The Closing of the American Mind,* Simon and Schuster, New York, 1987. Selected quotations (not in sequence).

5. The critical mass is not necessarily the majority of people. It is the minimum number of people whose commitment is necessary to break resistance to change.

6. A.P. Martin, *The Proactive Thinking Paradigm* Chapter III "Mission-setting and Review: The First Commandment of Business", The Professional Development Institute, 1995, Tel: (819) 772-7777.

7. B. Eugene Griessman, *The Achievement Factors:
    Candid Interviews with Some of the Most Successful
    People of Our Time,* Dodd, Mead & Co., New York,
    1987, p.123, ISBN 0-396-08977-1, $18.95.

8. A.P. Martin, *The Proactive Thinking Paradigm,*
    Chapter IV "How to Validate Objectives",
    The Professional Development Institute, 1995,
    Tel: (819) 772-7777.

Personal notes

_____

_____

_____

_____

_____

_____

_____

_____

_____

_____

_____

_____

_____

_____

_____

_____

_____

_____

_____

Section 3

Concentrate on priorities

Leverage your time the Proactive way

13. Determine priority before urgency.

Even with a clear mission and valid objectives, excessive workload and conflicting demands on our time and resources cannot be resolved without an effective means to set priority and urgency. Let us establish a thorough understanding of priority and urgency to lay the foundation for scheduling our day-to-day work.

There is no shortage of priority-setting schemes. Our approach takes into account the work of Drucker, Lakein and MacKenzie and it is described in detail in *The Proactive Thinking Paradigm*[1] from which the following excerpts are made.

Priority designates value, importance, weight and equity. Priority *is* relevance to mission. Priority *is not* urgency. It is the degree of a task's contribution to the mission of the organization. It is likely to be misunderstood and is often erroneously associated with urgency.

We tend to devote our prime time to tasks that are urgent and relatively easy to perform *rather than* to the important, high-priority work which often cannot be done without adequate thinking, planning and concentrated effort. As a result, our performance suffers.

The priority of a project or a program cannot automatically be passed down to its individual actions (or deliverables). Once the program priority is known, it is imperative to define the priority of each of its actions. Thus, the priority of an action will be defined as the relevance of that action to the program (or project).

Priorities are dynamic and temporary. They change as a result of shifts in mission boundaries, new risks or players (stakeholders), or as new objectives to fulfill the mission emerge. What is important today could become worthless tomorrow because both people and needs change constantly. Therefore:

• priority-setting should be *expeditious* i.e. done speedily and efficiently; and

• priority review exercises should be *frequent*.

There are five classes of priority:

1. Essential (E)
2. Important (I)
3. Marginal or Nice-to-have (N)
4. Unavoidable obligation (U)
5. Futile or fruitless (F)

The first three priorities are for *stay-in-business* work as opposed to *stay-out-of-trouble* work or unavoidable obligations. These priorities are applied to tasks that should make a *positive* contribution to the mission, that is:

• *revenue-generating* tasks (private sector) and programs providing a useful service (public sector); and

• *productivity improvement or cost-saving* activities or projects.

Priorities four and five apply to tasks and programs that are neither of the above but which are *imposed* on the organization through legislation, tradition, coercion or some idiosyncratic protocol. They could also be deliberately or inadvertently *self-inflicted*.

A task is **essential** when its completion is vital and critical to the fulfillment of the corporate mission. The success of the task would *add high value to the long-term performance* of your organization and to that of its allies. By the same token, its failure could permanently handicap your organization or its key allies and could severely jeopardize corporate performance.

A task is **important** when its completion is a determining factor in the fulfillment of either our corporate mission or that of our key allies. The success of the task would yield *high value to the short- and medium-term* but not necessarily to long-term performance. By the same token, its failure could temporarily handicap corporate performance, although the company could easily survive.

High leverage activities that affect the performance of a significant number of people should be considered at least **important** if not **essential** on the priority scale. These are the tasks that either help you gain or maintain a competitive edge or that affect the productivity of a significant number of people. Their deliverables include memos, order forms, procedure manuals, mechanical aids, jigs, fixtures, consumer goods, banknotes, coins, drivers' licences, credit cards, passports, postal codes, customs documents, compilers and computer systems which are intended for a large number of users. These tasks should be designed carefully to minimize processing time by users and to reduce the risk of misuse or misinterpretation.

At the personal level, a high leverage activity increases your capacity and ability to live better, to work smarter and to do more with less effort. High leverage activities are frequently undervalued because they are not an end in themselves. They are a means to an end. Skills training, planning and coaching others fall in this category if they increase your day-to-day effectiveness and ultimately your capacity to do better with less resources.

A task is **marginal** or **nice-to-have** when its contribution to the mission is minimal and its absence would not alienate key allies. *Nice-to-have* jobs should be discarded or treated as *fill-in* work and performed only during slack periods when the *must* work is unavailable. Here, *must* work refers to the essential and important jobs.

All of the above classes of priority refer to work that generates a revenue, provides a useful service or reduces costs. The next priorities refer to tasks that are a *drain* on corporate resources.

An **unavoidable obligation** is a task which cannot be classified as a revenue-generating or cost-saving activity, but which must be done to prevent serious adverse consequences to the organization or its key allies. Year-end tax returns, many compulsory activities and damage-control projects fall into this category. Unless one can convert these obligations into opportunities, such as saving on income tax, they should either be delegated to junior staff members or performed quickly with the *minimum effort* and preferably as *fill-in work* and outside prime time hours.

A **futile** or **fruitless** task belongs to the last class of priorities. It does not contribute to the mission of the organization nor to its key allies, and it lacks a worthwhile purpose. It should be either ignored altogether or quickly discarded through appeal to reason, prudent negotiations or the use of business acumen and managerial skills.

14. Define urgency without falling into its traps.

Urgency specifies delivery time or deadline. Urgency has a direct bearing on cost, which may be excessive when the program deadline is unquestionably passed down to its individual actions (or deliverables). This aberration is due to the deadline myth in our society and to the ignorance of the fact that the urgency of an objective, like its priority, should not be passed down automatically to every activity. One can cite hundreds of projects in which management resorted

to unnecessary overtime and to additional resources for
activities which were not operationally required prior
to the official project deadline.

It is unrealistic to have objectives without deadlines.
However, taking deadlines at face value is the source
of major inefficiencies in engineering, systems
development and production sites. Thus, we need to
differentiate between several types of urgency or deadline; each is a practical cutoff date for a specific
purpose or decision:

- official deadline (often ceremonial)

- operational or functional deadlines (there may
  be more than one)

- fiscal deadline for cashflow or tax purposes

- overall completion

The official cutoff date is frequently required for
strategic gains and may even be near the beginning of
the project to send the signal to competitors that the
project is launched and that they now should stay away.
A leading petrochemical manufacturer was interested
in building a plant for a special market segment, but
he was concerned about the competition. The limited
size of the market made it profitable for one plant, not
two. Our client would build his plant only if the competition was not ahead in its own planning. In order
to find out about the competition and, at the same time
face it with a *fait accompli,* he fenced and graded one
of his own vacated lots and arranged for a cocktail
party to celebrate the impending erection of the plant.
The competitors recognized that the market would only

sustain one plant and that our client *appeared sufficiently ahead* to thwart their plans to do the same. Thus, ceremonial deadlines can have a strategic value.

The ceremonial deadline could also be used to keep public pressure away from a politician or a sponsor. For this purpose, a fence or a building façade plus a pair of scissors and ribbons can be sufficient to stage a ceremony to send a clear message to the constituents that work is underway. In such cases, architecture and engineering can be performed at the right pace as they don't have to meet the ceremonial deadline.

The functional deadline corresponds to the date when essential deliverables are ready for day-to-day operations even though the project is not yet complete. In road construction projects, we try to complete the bridges first in order to get rid of the barges. Hydroelectric dams are turned on as soon as the turbines and the power lines are ready, even though the guard's house may still be under construction. Hotel owners open for business before the swimming pool is complete.

The fiscal deadline sets the time by which elements of a project should be complete in order to post their cost to the current fiscal year and then take advantage of depreciation or research tax credits.

The overall completion date is self-explanatory.

In summary, we should try to convert the *client deadline* into multiple deadlines and work to meet each deadline using *just-in-time* principles whenever the benefits of the *multiple-deadline* approach outweigh its cost.

15. Schedule and prune your workload constantly.

The above guidelines can be used to specify priority and urgency not only at the program or project level, but also at the task level and in your daily *do-list*. As an example, a task that is *essential (E)* and due the *8th week* would be coded *E8*.

Once identified, priority and urgency should be used to *rank* all essential, important jobs and unavoidable obligations. The objective is to prune our workload constantly in order to concentrate on one or two high leverage tasks or the best *bang for the buck*. To this end, we must again ask the *ever-present* question:

What is the best use of my time right now?

If the answer is known, we must go ahead and do the work. When the job is finished, we should not embark on the next task on the priority list but should repeat the above exercise *expeditiously*. This frequent review is not a time-waster but the best insurance to limit the perverse consequences of possible errors from previous decisions. It provides for a constant self-correcting mechanism in priority-setting, particularly when new assignments come and go quickly and unexpectedly.

Further insights on priority-setting can be found in *The Proactive Thinking Paradigm* and in an article by Professor Curtis H. Jones which offers valuable suggestions to establish priorities based on the return on our scarce time.[2]

16. Formulate viable strategies.

For each objective, consider all available options including the *wait-and-see* option, the *compliance* option (the minimum to get by), the *active* option (do what is expected) and the *proactive* option.

The proactive option focuses on seizing the opportunity promptly and on doing better with less.[3] Reserve this option for worthwhile goals of highest priority. Try to deliver more than you promise. Exceed your quotas. But don't try to be *proactive* with everyone; you could end up with a pacemaker!

17. Manage risk.

Don't speculate. Risk is everywhere. Assess the benefits and the risks associated with each of the above options before crafting a strategy. If the stakes are high and hostility is part of the risk, do not underestimate its adverse consequences. Prepare contingency plans and damage-control interventions for the worst-case scenario. You will never be sorry.

Risk management includes risk identification, risk estimation, risk mitigation or acceptance, and strategy implementation and control. The instruments for these tasks are beyond the scope of this discussion. They are the subject of a separate essay which includes a comprehensive bibliography on the topic.[4]

18. Break objectives into small tasks and milestones.

To this end, apply the principles of flow charting.[5]
Use the work breakdown structures and the work
definition instruments of the Global Method®.[6]

19. State targets to measure what matters.

A performance target or a milestone is an event within
or at the end of an activity where added value is either
visible or can be inferred from surrogate[7] measures of
progress and quality. Try to reach at least one major
milestone or complete one important objective each
week. If you cannot, try to make significant progress
on it.

20. Set specific time for scheduling every day.

Invest 10 minutes early in the morning (or the night
before) to review your progress and schedule your day
based on your weekly workload and daily events. For
this purpose, use a quiet area at home or in the office.
The questions for daily planning are:

- *What are my daily objectives and priorities?*
- *What should I delegate?*
- *When should I start working on each objective?*
- *For how long?*

21. Prepare daily *do-lists* with the Harvard Planner®.

Do not rely on your memory. Use your Harvard Planner®

for your personal and business planning needs. Always carry it with you.

Every day, ask yourself not only what you should do but also what things you should avoid, such as watching trivial TV programs or low-priority tasks.

Group your activities so that they reduce travel time, set-up costs and duplication of effort. Remember to block prime time for important tasks — those that increase your long term effectiveness. Set slack time for unforeseen opportunities and urgencies. Carry *light* work or reading materials in case of unexpected delays in airports or elsewhere.

Confirm before heading for a medical or business appointment to ensure that, upon arrival, you will not unduly wait for your turn. This initiative will save you several hours each year.

22. Avoid perfectionism on routine obligations.

Do the minimum to get by on routine statutory activities (e.g. income tax returns) and other obligations that neither serve your clients nor reduce your costs.

Set aside routine and minor tasks with low payoff. Act quickly on them during your *fill-in* time. Fill-in time is the opposite of *high-energy* prime time. It is the waiting time between meetings or important calls, or the low-energy time at the end of the day.

23. Be flexible.

Plans are meant to be changed as the situation dictates. They are not an end in themselves. Keep them simple. Avoid overengineering.

References and notes

1. A.P. Martin, *The Proactive Thinking Paradigm,* The Professional Development Institute, 1995, Tel: (819) 772-7777.

2. Curtis H. Jones, *The Money Value of Time,* Harvard Business Review, July-August 1968.

3. A.P. Martin, *Think Proactive,* Chapter 2, The Professional Development Institute, 1984, ISBN 0-86502-000-0, $24.

4. A.P. Martin, *Strategic Risk Management,* Paper presented at The Euro-American Conference on Project Management jointly sponsored by Internet (Europe) and PMI (USA) October, 1989 in Atlanta. Copies available from PDI, 70 Technology Blvd., Hull, Canada J8Z 3H8, $6.95.

5. For a concise description of flow charting and other instruments of work simplification and Total Quality Management, order your complimentary copy of *The Memory Jogger: A Pocket Guide of Tools for Continuous Improvement,* published by Goal/QPC, 13 Branch St., Methuen, MA 01844, 1988 edition, Tel: (508) 685-3900.

6. A.P. Martin, *How to Prepare a Work Breakdown Structure,* Volume 8, PDI Press, 1986, 70 Technology Blvd., Hull, Canada J8Z 3H8, $10.

7. A surrogate measure is a substitute for a direct measure of performance. Surrogate measures are frequently necessary to control the progress of complex projects such as R&D where traditional measures of earned value are not adequate.

Personal notes

Section 4

Reduce your workload

Increase your effectiveness

24. Invest your prime time in what you value most.

Value the quiet hour. Take advantage of your prime time – the time when you are most alert, creative and productive. Set aside a quiet hour at a fixed time daily. Others will learn to respect it. Invest the hour in planning, thinking and working with high payoff and high-leverage activities. Concentrate on these tasks to get meaningful results. If the office is noisy, use the library.

25. Give your total attention to one topic at a time.

High concentration on a single target is a learned skill. Select the time and place of each action carefully to readily gain access to the required people, tools, documents. Avoid interruptions and distractions. Meanwhile, if you think of anything unrelated to the *action in progress,* your energy is less focused and stress builds up from competing demands on the brain. This fragmentation of energy is dysfunctional and time-wasting. The solution is to quickly log the interfering ideas or errands in your Harvard Planner for future attention. Thus, your mind is freed up for the action in progress.

26. Avoid anarchy and constant interruptions.

Strike a balance between keeping your door open and closed. Limit open door policy to a specific hour in the day to avoid constant interruptions by staff and drop-in visitors. If you don't have an office door, post a sign such as *'Do not disturb'* or *'Please leave a message or come back at ...'.*

27. Don't be a jack-of-all-trades.

Let a skilled accountant do your tax returns and an experienced mechanic fix your car. Call on qualified workers (or students) to cut the lawn, remove the snow or paint the house unless you have the time and skills or find pleasure in performing these chores. Focus your energy where you can get the best return on your time.

28. Learn to say *no* even to your best friends.

Sometimes the best you can do for a friend is to withhold a favor. If the friendship is real, it will survive the incident and grow stronger. If not, it will break up anyway, perhaps the sooner the better.[1] For more on the topic, read the chapter *"How to Say 'No', Five Easy Ways"* by Robert Moskovitz[2].

Minimize overcommitments. If you value quality, you should neither seek nor accept more work than you can deliver on time. Say *no* earlier rather than later because once you have made a commitment, you could lose more money and time by cancelling it. Time is a finite resource. Saying *yes* to one demand means saying *no* to another. [3]

29. Commute wisely.

Try to reduce your commute time by living closer to work, working at home more often, changing your itinerary or using a car pool or public transportation. Use your commute time to relax or learn a skill on cassette. Join a car pool if it does not add to your travel time. Either share the driving or let a partner who enjoys the driving do it. This is how I read the daily paper when in my hometown.

30. Reduce your workload by making lasting decisions.

Your workload comprises a series of decisions and related actions. Whether they are made by you or by others, decisions that affect your time can be either explicit or can exist by default.

The longevity of a decision refers to the time during which a decision remains in effect. There is an inverse correlation between workload and decision longevity. That is, the shorter the decision's longevity, the greater the need for more decisions and the higher the workload. One cause of the constant increase in the workload of most organizations comes directly from the shortened life span of the decisions they now make.

Consider the interest rate charged by banks for personal or business loans. In the fifties, the decision was made about once or twice a year. A senior executive meeting was necessary to ratify such a decision in most banks.

Interest rates remained unchanged throughout the year. In the nineties, interest rate decisions are reviewed at least once a day and the demand for such decisions grew from a frequency of one to over 250 per year, at the rate of about one each working day. No bank executive can cope with such exponential growth in the demand for decisions. As a result, interest rate decisions had to be delegated from the executive suite to the professional economist. The role of the senior executive shifted from decision-making to policy-making. Instead of making decisions, the executive establishes the ground rules under which the decision should be made and gauges the corridor within which the professionals can freely operate.

What happened in banking and finance is gradually taking place in manufacturing. This trend is most visible in information technology. In the sixties, computers and related software were acquired for at least five years. A detailed five- to ten-year plan was common among the Fortune 500 companies. The shorter life span of current equipment and software partially accounts for the growing workload of purchasing agents and systems professionals.

In consumer goods, the hairdryer introduced by GE in the fifties lasted years before the competition caught up with it. Today, a six-month reprieve is a blessing. The same drift is affecting defence, medicine and unregulated industries.

Even in our private lives, the downward slope in the longevity of marriages and partnerships has led to a higher workload for individuals, lawyers, accountants, movers and courts.

If you are genuinely interested in decreasing your workload, consider the longevity of the decisions you make. The greater the life span of your decisions, the lighter your workload.

Naturally, there are exceptions. Interest rates are volatile by necessity. Bank economists have no choice but to respond to the market demands.

Despite the trend toward perishable decisions for society at large, you can, at your level, make more lasting decisions by:

- nurturing and consolidating your relationship with your spouse and family;
- staying very close to your customers, staff and suppliers;
- negotiating longer contract periods;
- not compromising on quality and customer service;
- giving preference to promotions from within; and
- sparing no effort to build trust with everyone in your industry including the competition.

When the pressure for frequent decisions cannot be reversed, consider pre-programmed decisions or delegation as outlined below.

31. Value pre-programmed decisions.

Value pre-programmed decisions when they can lead

to speedy, unambiguous and precise actions. A greater appreciation of strategic and operational policies should provide a framework for substantial time savings and for delegation of operating decisions. Quick action and better results are among the payoffs, as illustrated in the following examples.

A leading pharmaceutical company spent endless regular hours and a large dose of overtime studying and formulating individual responses to Requests for Proposals (RFP) with limited success. The generic drug manufacturers were gradually siphoning its market share. Using Professor Michael Porter's paradigm[4] and *Factional Analysis*[5], the company built a framework to speed up the bidding process by focusing on high potential clients. It decided to decline work for marginal clients (not marginal bids) whenever possible and bid high when bidding was mandatory for these clients. Within three months, the company's success rate on bids went up. Nine months later, it recovered the share it had lost in that market segment.

The same approach has been recommended and implemented in a number of government agencies. Our work with the International Development Agency provided its executives with a framework to assess the Federal Government's response to individual countries' pleas for technical and humanitarian assistance. Rather than react to each request, the Agency identified a socio-econographic profile of the developing world. Socio-econographics are the institutional equivalent of psychographics for individuals. All countries were ranked with respect to their socioeconomic attributes. Thus, Algeria and Venezuela, at the time, were *revenue-*

rich, technology-poor and moderate in basic infrastructure. Brazil was *revenue-poor, technology-secure and self-sufficient on basic infrastructure.*

The Agency went on to allocate its resource time and dollars on the basis of maximizing the impact of its contribution using these attributes. Thereafter, officers spent less time assessing requests and more time providing valued assistance in the field.

References and notes

1. The comments about friendship were based on a personal conversation with my friend and mentor Richard Beckhard before he retired from The Alfred Sloan School of Management, Massachusetts Institute of Technology.

2. Robert Moskovitz, "How to Say 'No', Five Easy Ways" in *How to Organize Your Work and Your Life: Proven Time Management Techniques for Business Professionals and other Busy People,* DoubleDay, New York, p. 270, ISBN 0-385-17012-2, $10.95.

3. Andrew S. Grove, *High-Output Management: The President of Intel, one of the Nation's Premier High Technology Companies, Shows How Managers Can Increase Their Productivity Dramatically,* Random House, New York, 1983, p.64, ISBN 0-394-53234-1, $16.95.

4. Michael Porter's profound contribution to the field of strategy formulation is reflected in several books and video cassettes. Among the recommended readings:

   Competitive Strategy: Techniques for Analyzing Industries and Competitors, The Free Press, Collier Mac-Millan Publishing Co., New York, 1980, ISBN 0-02-925360-8, $29.

Competitive Advantage, The Free Press, 1985.

The Competitive Advantage of Nations, The Free Press, 1990, ISBN 0-02-925361-6, $35.

Highly recommended viewing includes:

Michael Porter on Competitive Strategy, 2 tapes, Harvard Business School Video Series, Soldiers Field, Boston, MA 02163.

The Competitive Advantage of Nations in two versions: private sector and government, 4 tapes each, also from Harvard Business School Video series.

5. A.P. Martin, *The Proactive Thinking Paradigm,* Chapter II "The Change-makers," The Professional Development Institute, 1995.

Personal notes

_____

_____

_____

_____

_____

_____

_____

_____

_____

_____

_____

_____

_____

_____

_____

_____

_____

_____

_____

_____

Section 5

Think teamwork

Delegate & seek help

32. Understand the driving forces of your workload.

Think of your daily workload as the product of a series
of interacting variables including:

1. The demands on your time
   - demands related to your job and its
     environment;
   - demands related to your health and lifestyle;
   - demands related to your family and social
     interests; and
   - demands resulting from surprise events.

2. The available time and your capability to deal with
   the above demands. Capability includes your know-
   how, technology, communication tools and the
   power to mobilize and allocate resources to respond
   to the demands on your time.

In order to improve your performance, you have to
work on these variables. The previous sections offered
valuable tips for that purpose. This section provides

further insights into an important topic: delegation as a means to handle your daily workload. The objective is to train our subordinates, colleagues and children to solve their own problems.

Delegation is not only a management tool. It is a timesaving instrument available to all of us, both at work and at home. Even neighbors and their children can help you take care of errands, snow removal and other obligations. Reciprocate when they need your help. Thus, everyone saves time.

33. Don't delegate what you can eliminate.

Think work simplification before work delegation. General Electric's *Work-Out* process is among the best frameworks for eliminating non-value added work. G.E. states that *Work-Out* is:

> . . . used across GE to involve the leaders of every business unit in a dialogue to identify positive steps to improve and streamline work processes. Typical sessions begin with the business leader spending a half-day with the group describing and discussing the competitive realities and challenges facing the business. The group then divides into teams for one day to produce proposals that value speed, simplicity, and self-confidence. At the end of the session, each team presents its proposal. Every idea receives a response, and many of the proposals are adopted on the spot during the presentation.

Information on *Work-Out* is now widely available.[1] Try a pilot experiment before implementing it throughout your organization. If well integrated to your own culture, it will add to your productivity and create more rewarding jobs.

Don't delegate time-wasters. Avoid handing over piecemeal work to people who can take over the complete assignment or project. Delegate valued activities that can be done more economically and more efficiently by others. I taught my daughter to balance my chequebook and to help with shopping when she was a young teenager. At 19, she selected, test-drove and negotiated the purchase of my new car. This first experience of buying a new car for the family was challenging and enjoyable for her. For me, it saved many hours, not to mention the stress induced by such a transaction.

34. Consider the skill level.

The skills and experience of your subject affect the nature and complexity of the assignment to be delegated. According to Dr. Abrahmson, Vice-President of American Express Travelers' Division: "The development stages through which a person acquires a skill are:

Stage 1: Novice

The novice is a beginner without experience who needs assistance to decompose the assignment into manageable activities. Give the beginner rules for determining action and provide monitoring and feedback.

Stage 2: Proficient

The proficient comes with an increased practice that exposes one to a whole variety of situations. Issue recognition is not performed by calling attention to recurrent sets of features but rather by singling out perspicuous examples. The proficient can recognize risk and has the know-how to correct these conditions.

Stage 3: Expert

The repertoire of experienced situations by the expert is so vast that the occurrence of a specific situation intuitively triggers an appropriate action.

Stage 4: Master

With conscious self-monitoring, the expert no longer needs to develop constant attention to performance. Thus, energy is devoted only to identifying appropriate perspective and actions.''

35. Delegate gradually by apprenticeship.

Keep in mind the double-edged dilemma of inadequate delegation. Giving subordinates less work or responsibility than they are prepared to cope with can be frustrating and time-wasting. By the same token, delegating responsibility, especially to newcomers, is easy. But asking them to relinquish it is not. Thus, delegation must be gradual and based on skill level, commitment and trust, as well as on the following options compiled from notes taken while attending a seminar on *Consulting Skills* conducted by Dr. Sam Abrahmson:

* *Gather facts only:*

    Ask your subject to look into the problem, to get you all the facts and you decide what to do.

* *Identify the options:*

    Ask your subject to gather the facts, identify the different options and to let you know the pros and cons of each. You decide.

* *Recommend a course of action:*

    In addition to generating options, ask your subject to make recommendations for your approval.

* *Submit for approval:*

    Ask your subject to let you know what he/she intends to do and to withhold action until you approve.

* *Take action and communicate results:*

    Ask your subject to let you know what he/she did and what happened.

* *Take action and communicate only failure*

- *It's all yours:*

  This is total delegation. The subject takes action
  and no further communication with you is
  necessary.

36. Provide excellent support.

Empower your team and family members to promptly
get the tools, the information and the resources to do
the job and assess their own performance. State clearly
what you expect. Encourage initiative, self-help and
risk-taking. Train subordinates to undertake speedy
actions, preferably at the front line. Set realistic deadlines
and quality standards. Coach for high performance.

37. Monitor results.

Provide and seek ongoing feedback. Let people know
how they are doing and reciprocally, insist on a candid
assessment of your own performance. Studies show
evidence that our belief in another person's ability is
an important element of that person's performance.[2]

38. Discuss the specific shortcomings.

Don't point the finger at anyone. Tolerate accidental
and unintentional failures. Focus on continuous
improvement opportunities when discussing
shortcomings, be specific and helpful.

39. Reward fairly and praise generously.

Rewards are perceptual. Many are transitory. What

counts is what the recipient expects and values now. Consider non-monetary rewards. Honest praise is essential, but not always sufficient. One way to find out what your subordinates value is to observe their behavior. Note their comments and any feedback from others that may provide revealing signs about their most cherished wants, wishes and desires. Cultivate empathy. Validate before you act.

40. Stay lean. Build lasting alliances.

Keep a small nucleus of dedicated, versatile and skilled staff. Call on reliable outside help to handle both planned and unexpected upsurges in workload. Save time by building trust and a lasting alliance with key suppliers and temporary personnel who know your environment and needs.

John Pepper, President of Procter & Gamble, credits part of the company's success to its long-standing association with its staff, retailers and suppliers. In an interview with Professor Michael Porter of the Harvard Business School, Mr. Pepper indicated that his company has worked with the same advertising agency for 67 years.[3]

41. Invest in your ultimate freedom.

Prepare for your succession as early as possible. There is no faster way to increase your domain of action and chances of upward mobility.

42. Question your behavior.

Refrain from wasting the time of others. Respect their right to manage their time as you wish them to respect yours.

References and notes

1. For more on General Electric's *Work-Out,* read:

    Noel Tichy and Ram Charan, *Speed, Simplicity and Self-Confidence,* Harvard Business Review, N° 89513, Sept.-Oct. 89.

    GE Money Machine: How its Emphasis on Performance Built a Colossus of Finance, Business Week, March 8, 1993, p. 62.

    or contact: GE Crotonville, P.O. Box 368, Croton-on-Hudson, NY 10520, Tel: (914)944-2136.

2. Norman C. Hill, *How to Increase Employee Competence,* McGraw-Hill Book Co., New York, 1984, p. 56, ISBN 0-07-028790-2.

3. For more on Michael Porter's interview, order the *Competitive Strategy* video cassette from the Harvard Business School Video Series, Soldiers Field, Boston, MA 02163.

Personal notes

_____

_____

_____

_____

_____

_____

_____

_____

_____

_____

_____

_____

_____

_____

_____

_____

_____

_____

Section 6

Organize your space

Use the best time savers

43. Arrange your working area.

Apply the proven concepts of ergonomics[1] to make
your workplace more effective and safer for everyone.
Place your desk, filing cabinet, computer and telephone
to minimize distraction and redundant movements. Use
an ergonomic chair. If you can afford it, add a stand-up
desk and occasionally use it to reduce fatigue. Streamline your hand movements and simplify your body
motions to increase productivity and comfort.
Inadequate lighting and excessive noise can greatly
decrease your productivity and cause safety and health
hazards.

On the wall facing you, place a clock as a constant
reminder of time. The clock is important to help us
schedule and regulate the pace of work, since our
biological clock tends to be slower than the official
clock, as Bruno Jarroson documented in his profound
essay on the meaning of time.[2]

If you work even sporadically from home, read Paul
and Sarah Edwards' publications on the topic. Both

authors offer new insights and tips about outfitting
your home office with furnishings and supplies, about
lighting and noise control.[3]

44. Don't compromise on stationery.

Keep a good supply of pens, pencils, paper,
highlighters, staplers and rulers on hand. If you use
pencils, have your own electric pencil sharpener. If you
are in North America, buy 7-hole punches. They are
good for both 3- and 7-hole sheets. With 7-ring binders,
you can use regular thickness paper which is environ-
mentally friendly and weighs half as much as the 3-hole
paper stock for equal binding strength.[4]

When balancing your chequebook or travel expenses,
use a calculator with a paper roll or a palm-top
computer to log your computations. You will be able
to trace mistakes, if any, more quickly.

45. Shop for the best time savers.

Don't believe conventional wisdom. Time savers are
not necessarily expensive, particularly when they last
much longer than their cheaper counterparts. Consider
the space pens originally designed for use during the
moon-landing mission of NASA.[5] They write at any
angle. They never leak and their cartridge outlasts
regular pens by three times. Yet, they now cost less than
famous brands. Voice-activated or magnetic door keys,
remote-control switches for electrical appliances and
lights, openers for garage doors and smart phones with
hand-free sets are well worth their cost.

Buy light and sturdy briefcases and suitcases that are patented as genuine time savers. I found a black canvas briefcase that is ultralight and rain-resistant, with several compartments, key holders, reinforced built-in straps for heavy loads of books, all for a mere $30!

For more on stationery, consult Susan Silver's book *Organized To Be Best*. It is among the well-researched publications on office configurations, office equipment and supplies, including colored folders, divider tabs, binders, display boards and mobile stands.[6]

46. Think prevention and unconditional warranties.

Everybody has something to sell. Validate claims with credible references. Request unconditional warranties in writing on expensive items. The market place is full of miracle products, books and seminar providers claiming to turn clients into experts in just one day. In purchasing, prevention is better than cure.

47. Integrate time into all your buying decisions.

Major purchasing policies and daily shopping should comprise time saving as a cardinal rule. Make intelligent buying decisions that should reward you for many years to come.

Use standing offers and blanket orders instead of negotiating each deal. Thus, you save time involved in negotiation and you can take advantage of the economy of scale of multiple orders. In our Institute, we offer our major customers, including the Federal Government, the mutual benefits of extending contracts from one to three years on specific office products. As a result, suppliers and customers can plan on a longer horizon and focus on service quality instead of devoting excessive time to bidding and negotiating tactics.

48. Plan and cluster your purchases.

Shopping takes time. Do it wisely. Use catalogues for durable products and consumer goods. Order by phone or by fax from reputable suppliers who offer a money-back guarantee and extended manufacturer's warranty. If you wish to pick up a product, call in advance to confirm the detailed address, office hours and directions because most companies are not static. They grow, restructure or move.

Stock up on clothing, shoes, toiletries and food (e.g. powdered milk). Look for quality and durability in a product. Germany's *Bama Lam* leather boots won awards for quality, durability and design aesthetics. Priced competitively, they can last ten Canadian winters.

Avoid window shopping and weekend line-ups. Set a time limit. Stick to your plan. You will save money, time and frustration in the long term. On the way home from the office, I usually shop every second month for all but perishable food which I pick up once a week.

49. Don't clutter your desk.

Keep everything in a state of readiness. Tools, stationery and furniture should always be clean, ready for use and in the right place. Discard brochures, memos and documents either of marginal value or without a clear and legitimate purpose. Other documents and memos should be either forwarded to the appropriate staff or filed even temporarily. Anything you do not need for the action currently in progress should be removed from the working surface of your desk. Place it in a nearby drawer or a filing cabinet, on a shelf or a credenza that is within arm's reach.

Tidy your desk whenever you leave the office. You will appreciate it when you return. "With an organized, efficient desk, you can save both time and money. Fewer things will slip through the cracks. You can stay on top of your unfinished work, locate your paper and files within seconds, and become more productive."[7]

50. Think security.

Safeguard your valuable files and confidential materials. Don't leave terminals and work stations active while you are away. Lock up or log out. Protect your assets (car, home) with the best security system. New wireless technology can protect your office, car and home at a fraction of the cost of traditional systems.[8]

Use a laser marker to clearly indicate at least your phone number on your palm- or laptop computer. You should also securely glue your business card to the machine. It is aggravating, and sometimes impossible, for local police and airlines to trace the identity of the owner of a computer that is either found or collected from a thief. A recent broadcast indicated that last year over 670 personal computers were not claimed from lost-and-found counters in airports, buses, schools and hotels.

Everyday, municipal police across North America recover stolen compact disk players, but can't locate their owners.

51. Back up your Harvard Planner® and valuable documents.

Plan to back up your calendar regularly. I meet at least two executives each year who have lost their Planner due to negligence or theft. File the back-up copies in alternate areas that are accessible, secure and safe.

References and notes

1. As defined by Susan Silver, "Ergonomics is the science
    of making the work environment compatible with
    people so they can work more comfortably and produc-
    tively. Ergonomics looks at the dimensions of work
    tables, desks and chairs and matches them to the wide
    range of body sizes and shapes . . . . When you pay
    close attention to these standards you can avoid such
    symptoms as fatigue, eyestrain, blurred vision,
    headaches, stiff muscles, irritability and loss of feelings
    in fingers and wrists." For more insights into
    ergonomics and time management, read *Organized To
    Be Best!* by Susan Silver and available from either your
    local bookstore or directly from Adams-Hall
    Publishing, Box 491002, Los Angeles, CA 90049,
    Tel:(310) 826-1851 or 1-800-888-4452.

2. Like *Time Wars* by Jeremy Rifkin, the book *Briser la
    dictature du temps*, by Bruno Jarroson is in a class by
    itself. It is an invitation to question our deeply-held
    beliefs about the myopia of efficiency and the meaning
    of several dimensions of our personal and collective
    time. It is published in French by Maxima, éditeur
    Laurent du Mesnil, Paris, 1993, ISBN 2-84001-027-5.

3. No one working even sporadically at home can afford
    to ignore Paul and Sarah Edwards' timesaving tips.
    Many ideas can also be applied effectively in the
    corporate office:

Paul & Sarah Edwards, *Working from Home: Everything You Need to Know about Living and Working Under the Same Roof,* 4th. Revised Edition, Tarcher/Putnam, New York, ISBN 0-87477-582-5, Tel:1-800-788-6262, $14.95.

4.   Vinyl and leather binders with six or seven rings should be available from your local office stationers. If not, they can be ordered in bulk quantities from PDI at (819) 772-7777.

5.   NASA Space Pens are available from PDI, 70 Technology Blvd., Hull, Canada J8Z 3H8, Tel: (819) 772-7777.

6.   Susan Silver, *Organized to be Best,* see first reference above.

7.   Jeffrey J. Mayer, *If you haven't the time to do it right, when will you find the time to do it over?* Simon & Schuster, New York, 1991, p.23.

8.   Charles Anton, *Technology Update,* Sept.-Oct. '93 issue, 2820 Waterford Lake Drive, Suite 106, Midlothian, Virginia 23113.

Personal notes

_____

_____

_____

_____

_____

_____

_____

_____

_____

_____

_____

_____

_____

_____

_____

_____

_____

_____

_____

_____

_____

Section 7

Cut down on paperwork

Value productive technology

52. Avoid the incoming mail and fax traps.

Are frequent deliveries of internal mail helping or hampering your performance? Can you do with one or two deliveries per day? Multiple deliveries are among the sources of interruptions cited by our clients. Even if you cannot change your company practices, consider the net benefits of handling your mail no more than once or twice a day. Train your assistant to at least scan and sort your mail by priority and urgency and to recommend solutions or take action where feasible.

Process incoming correspondence at once in the following manner. Throw away what you don't need. For the remainder, identify priority and urgency (planned start/finish), then consolidate immediately into the following electronic or hard-cover files:

- Immediate action - Personal work for this week, sorted by half-day;
- For immediate delegation or discussion;
- For activities that are due on a given date, use a *tickler system* which can be in the form of daily

(1-31), monthly or bi-monthly files from January to December – I found a monthly file system plus one folder for the current week sufficient for my needs;

– Archive - project files;

– Archive - client, supplier or staff files or legal/regulatory documents; and

– Scrap files - keep two files to be purged every quarter on a revolving basis.

As a safety precaution, I keep routine memos in the scrap file for three months before discarding them in the waste basket. I also retain in this file receipts from automatic teller machines just in case they don't show up in the bank statement.

Except for the scrap file, do not file a document before indexing it and logging the required action and the file reference in your Harvard Planner®. That way, you don't have to sift through the files endlessly. Use color coding to speed up archiving and tracing misplaced files.

53. Handle each document only once.

Discard useless and unwanted mail promptly. Reduce memo writing to the absolute minimum. If possible, call, fax or E-Mail the reply, or write it directly on the letter received and mail it back.

54. Dictate or write letter outlines only.

Let your secretary draft the content. Consider using a dictating machine particularly now that the ultralight recorder fits in a pocket. With a few months' practice, you can dictate fifteen times faster than you can write. Variable speech-control dictaphones now use speech-compression features to playback a cassette in half the time without loss in the audio-quality of the message.

55. Avoid buzzwords.

Cut empty phrases.[1] Brevity pays off. Restrict the use of plastic words, i.e. words that have a high power of connotation and a low power of designation such as development, information, empowerment, structure, communication and modernization. Plastic words tend either to cloud your message or add only marginal value to it.

Make an effort to use plain English terms. If the phrase or the word you use is not in a paperback dictionary such as the Webster's pocket edition, either avoid it or define it in the text or a footnote. Keep in mind that the use of jargon is a hostile act when addressing non-experts.

56. Learn to type. It is never too late.

Or, let a professional typist do it for you. Use the spelling-check features to save time.

If you have teenagers, send them on a typing course, the sooner the better. Within a couple of months, you will notice higher productivity in the preparation of school reports and other assignments. Ultimately, voice-activated data entry will replace typing but we are still a long way from making it reliable, affordable, simple and truly effective.

57. Speed up tracking your plans and work.

Managers and professionals spend endless hours looking for documents because of missing dates or identifiers. Always indicate the full date, including the year, both in daily correspondence and in routine notes. In addition, both your draft and final memos and reports should display in a non-obtrusive manner, preferably at the bottom of the page and in small print, the author's and typist's initials, the document name, the file reference and the computer drive code, if any (e.g. disk 3). In this way, all documents are accessible by anyone at any time. However, the time-saving need should not be at the expense of security. Confidential passwords should be used when required.

58. Move away from ad-hoc activities.

Consider programmed responses to repetitive demands. Use prerecorded audio messages or personalized form letters. Make sure the programmed response is prompt, straightforward and courteous.

59. Help your readers save time.

Write legibly. Avoid excessive reverse printing, half-tones and small print sizes. Think of the elderly and the shortsighted. Make reading pleasant for everyone. Design forms with enough space for the respondents to write comfortably. Insist on it as a customer as I have done with banks, credit card companies and governments.

60. Create documents that provoke a lasting impression.

Use the powerful features of desk top publishing and typesetting for widely distributed documents, letters and forms. Also take advantage of high density fonts to reduce the number of pages per document. Typesetting provides better quality, appearance and readability than common typing. Think colors, pictograms, illustrations and photography when the added value outweighs their cost.

If you are writing a mass distribution book, report or brochure, you can harness the capabilities of offset printing. With proper file preparation, you can produce negatives which require no manual intervention (stripping). Thus, you save time and money in pre-press activities and streamline the manufacturing process in building books, brochures and reports.[2]

61. Automate cautiously.

Integrate *decision-support systems* with sound managerial judgement. Mechanize routine tasks. Use the best available graphic aids for estimating, scheduling, budgeting and resource allocation. Plan and control projects with proven methods and effective software.

Consider the benefits of electronic mail services like CompuServe, AT&T Mail and MCI Mail. Products such as WinComPRO have pre-defined scripts that give you instant point and click access to electronic mail services and on-line data banks such as Dow Jones Investor Network (DJIN) and NewsNet.

62. Run computers and software wisely.

Avoid using machines without a thorough study of user manuals. With computer-aided graphics, in less than an hour our staff can make what took about two-hundred hours only five years ago. They are using the full repertoire of the programming software, unlike most users of the same product in our town who use less than ten percent of the machine's capability and complain about its complexity. But, it took us almost six months of training to harness the power of the new graphic arts system.

63. Value productive technology.

But remember, technology is perishable! Today's time-saver could be tomorrow's time-waster. Complacency is our worst adversary. Keep current. Act promptly but don't rush. Experiment to assess the real benefits, costs and risks.

References and notes

1. Dianna Booher, *Cutting Paperwork in the Corporate Culture,* Facts on File Publications, New York, 1986, ISBN 0-8160-1343-8.

2. For a seminar on *Electronic Page Processing, Pre-Press Savings and Book Manufacturing,* call BookCrafters, P.O. Box 370, 613 E. Industrial Dr., Chelsea, Michigan 48118, 1-800-999-BOOK (U.S. only) or (313) 475-9145, Fax: (313) 475-7337.

Personal notes

Section 8

Subject the phone to the bottom line

64. Take advantage of smart phones and cellular technology.

Although smart phone technology is now affordable, relatively few users are harnessing its great power. Many systems are simply not user friendly. Each brand has its own instruction protocol. A straight call-forwarding transaction or a three-way conference call requires different icons or push buttons from one system to another. While waiting for international standards, manufacturers can go a long way by simply writing basic user instructions on a self-adhesive plastic card located under the apparatus.

Unless you do your homework, your investment may be counterproductive. The James Martin group publishes up-to-date documentation on the topic and offers advanced seminars on data communications.[1] As a productivity primer for users, consider George Walther's *Phone Power*.[2] It includes practical tips for professionals, managers, receptionists and secretaries.

The useful features of current technology include call forwarding, speaker phones with handsfree and mute buttons, headsets, three-way conferencing, speed dialing, timers and message displays. Invest a few minutes to learn what is in it for you. Use universal headsets to speed up your performance and to avoid neck pain.[3]

If you opt for a telephone answering machine, consider one which permits you to give the callers of your choice a secret code. Instead of leaving a message, these callers will either access a confidential voice mailbox or contact you in your office or via your call forwarding feature. Instead of a beeper, your answering machine should also permit you to use a password for remote access. The small Code-a-Phone machine from Radio-Shack may suit your phone-answering needs if you constantly have to carry it, or if space is at a premium. If you expect a large volume of incoming calls, consider *call forwarding* or *voice mail* which can process several calls simultaneously. Your greeting message should be concise and courteous such as: *"Thank you for calling The Harvard Planner Group. Please leave a detailed message with your name, number and the best time to call you back."*

If you require a cellular phone, use it wisely. I keep one in my briefcase for reaching clients from airports and taxicabs and for reschedulings due to delays and emergencies. I also use it to call without leaving the car at night and to report accidents on the road. Only two people know my cellular phone number and they don't call it more than twice a year! Avoid using your cellular phone while driving. If you must do it frequently, consider the voice-activated dialing and handsfree speaker features.

A good pager can be a lifesaver. A poorly-selected one can turn into a time and money waster for the unwary. But if you really don't need it, leave it alone. Avoid pagers without digital caller identification or the area coverage you need. Motorola has brought a constant stream of innovative and advanced pagers to the market place. Its *Memo Express* can display a scrolling endless line of alphanumeric messages. The *Confident Pager* is a slim high-quality pager nicknamed the *Credit card*. Finally, *Encore* is a light numeric display pager that features a beeper which can also vibrate. Ask your phone company or Motorola at 1-800-548-9954 for a catalogue to learn more about the wide variety of pagers before making a hasty decision.

65. Schedule and consolidate your calls.

Pick the most convenient time for you and your respondent. Make the important calls during your prime time when you feel most alert. Return routine and easy calls when your energy is low. If you prefer to leave a message rather than talk to a correspondent who has voice mail, consider calling off-hours or during lunch time.

66. Reduce time spent looking for phone numbers.

How much of your day is spent looking for addresses or phone numbers? Managers (without secretaries) who monitor their time with the *Harvard® Time Log* are surprised to know that they waste ten minutes a day, or over one full week of productivity each year, in this disheartening task.

Use phone-dialer software to dial faster. Consider automatic number identifier features such as CallerID, which can help you identify the caller in order to decide whether it is worth your time to take the call.

Your letters should include both your phone and fax numbers as well as the phone and fax numbers of the receiver to speed up your follow-up calls and reduce errors. Record the receiver's numbers either below the reference line or in the top right corner of the letter. If your letterhead indicates the general company number, record your individual number or extension below your name and signature, when feasible.

67. Don't invite trivial work.

If you are getting unwanted or unsolicited calls at home, ask your phone company for a confidential number. At work, remove your phone and fax numbers from outgoing bulk letters and memos when no personal contact is preferred.

68. Handle incoming calls skillfully.

For expected calls, have the supporting documents and a note pad at your fingertips. Prepare your reply or questions in advance. If the call is important, let your receptionist and staff know so that you don't miss it, and spell the caller's name for them. They should greet the caller with: "Thanks for calling, Ms. Jones. I'll connect you to Mr. Martin who is expecting your call." For other calls, introduce yourself and, in a courteous way, ask the caller to do the same.

Avoid distraction. Give your full attention to the caller. If you can't, state why and suggest a better time. Find out the purpose of the call by asking questions that will help you process it promptly and effectively. If you are taking notes, say so. Confirm your understanding of the caller's requirements. Indicate what you are going to do and when the caller should expect a delivery or an answer. Make sure you follow-up on it.[4]

69. Be polite and brief.

Telemarketers know that a positive attitude on the phone is absolutely critical to their success. For all of us, it can go a long way toward developing excellent working relationships. With some of our clients, it has been the prelude for lasting friendships. Praise and thank anyone kind or helpful on the phone, particularly secretaries and support staff. Let their boss know, if appropriate.

Bring calls to a friendly but speedy conclusion. Use a graceful, empathic exit phrase. When you are unable to reach someone on the phone, leave a message with the purpose of the call, the information needed, and the best time to return the call.

70. Log your incoming messages.

Have an electronic system or a message book for your incoming calls. When you are out, leave your message book with your receptionist. Whether it is manual or electronic, a message book is a very powerful traffic and time log. Analyze the contents of the book at least once a year to detect traffic patterns and trends. If you are about to automate, consider computer systems using electronic pens and high-resolution flat screens.

71. Work in pairs.

Work in pairs if you don't have a receptionist or an electronic machine to answer your phone. Find someone with whom you can alternate and share the burden of phone answering.

References and notes

1. James Martin's seminars are among the best in the world on all aspects of communication technology including voice, data, video and multimedia. They are managed by Extended Intelligence Inc., 25 East Washington Street, Suite 600, Chicago, Illinois 60602, Tel. (312) 346-5245.

2. George Walther, *Phone Power,* Berkley Books, 1993, $4.50.

3. For universal headsets that can be plugged into your telephone system, contact your local phone company before ordering from manufacturers such as Plantronics at 1-800-544-4660.

4. John Cleese, *Telephone Behavior: The Power & The Perils,* Video Arts, 4088 Commercial Avenue, Northbrook, Illinois 60062,Tel: (312) 291-1008.

Personal notes

Section 9

Run productive meetings

72. Question the need and frequency of meetings.

What benefits would you expect from the meeting? Would a phone call or a memo do the job better or worse? Consider the use of teleconferencing in lieu of face-to-face meetings. Differentiate between information-sharing sessions or training seminars and meetings for problem solving (or issue management). Individual preparation is essential for problem-solving meetings. Otherwise, time-wasting occurs.

73. Know your audience.

Who should participate and why? Consider the vested interest, the role and the background of each participant. What value do they bring and what is in it for everyone?

Think about your credibility and the stakes before accepting a role in any meeting. If you are invited to deliver a speech or a presentation, do not underestimate preparation time. Are you invited out of courtesy? What real benefits would your participation bring to the audience? Consider declining the invitation if your participation is merely an investment in personal ego. Spare the time for something of lasting value.

74. Use the *Meeting Form* of The Harvard Planner®.

Use the *Meeting Form* of The Harvard Planner® for both planned and impromptu meetings. Available in desk, medium and pocket sizes, it permits you to quickly plan the meeting and promptly log each conclusion before discussing the next item on the agenda.

75. Plan meetings carefully.

Validate the objectives and agenda. Designate a leader and a recorder for formal meetings. Define the role of each participant with respect to each item on the meeting agenda:

- Who should be responsible for each topic?
- Who should approve or veto it?
- Who provides expertise or support?
- Who should attend the meeting for training purposes or merely to be informed?
- Who should be informed about each decision after the meeting?

If you are interviewing, don't improvise. Prepare for it ahead or postpone the interview. Reverse roles. Get help or take a seminar on the topic if you are a novice. Both recruiting and media interviewing are high-leverage activities.

76. Select the best date and location for the participants.

Reserve space. Think of the convenience and cost of accommodation, meals, airport shuttles, parking and ground transportation. Sometimes location is part of the incentive to attend. If appropriate, invite family members who can benefit from the learning experience or the trip.

77. Choose visuals that promptly get your message across.

Visuals can increase the retention value of the spoken message by a factor of five. Color pictures offer the best value followed by pictograms, graphs (line charts, pie charts and bar charts) and text (short phrases in bullet-point form). Make sure the visuals are legible, appealing and concise. Prepare hand-outs. Distribute them at the most appropriate time so that attendees don't read while you speak.

78. Simulate alternative scenarios.

Major conferences and corporate meetings with participants from different regions or countries should not be planned without due regard for the best and worst scenarios. Use devil's advocates. Think of alternate speakers just in case. Prepare contingency and damage control plans. Do not underestimate logistical problems with customs, brokers, freight carriers, over-night couriers, flight delays, room setup and delegates' registrations. Seek experienced help. If you fail, don't blame it on others.

79. Rehearse.

Use a TV camcorder or even a mirror in order to
practice before addressing a large audience or speaking
on an important issue. Check the timing. Stand on the
left of the projector and as close to the screen as
possible. Use a pointer to track your message. Don't
talk to the visuals as many presenters do. Face the
audience and speak up. Ask if your voice is heard by
everyone. Assess your performance. Seek candid feedback to continually improve your delivery style.

80. Avoid the last minute rush.

Beat the traffic, arrive earlier. But if you cannot, it is
essential to let your party know as early as possible.

81. Start meetings on time.

Don't penalize those who are punctual. Distribute the
agenda and pertinent material in advance. Limit the
meeting duration by subjecting each item on the agenda
to its own deadline. Schedule short breaks when the
duration exceeds an hour.

At the beginning of each meeting, try to let the people
know the time you are granting them even if the
gathering is informal or impromptu. By the same
token, indicate how much time you require from others
whenever you need their time. This practice can help
you save time and focus on the important issue right
away.

82. Start with important issues.

First, discuss important issues that build consensus. Finish with unpleasant and divisive topics. Listen and pay constant attention to verbal and non-verbal signals. Express yourself honestly.

83. Value the power of silence.

Whenever an important issue is brought up during a meeting, request a moment of silence to permit everyone to reflect on it without outside interference. Only then can you engage in a productive dialogue with a clear mind. By the same token, "don't be afraid of silence when you're waiting for an answer; people may need time to think about what's being discussed and how it affects them."[1] Listen and give your full attention to clearly understand the message of each participant. A greater synergy will result.

84. Stay on course. Orchestrate a genuine dialogue.

When seeking ideas, withhold the critiques until all suggestions are heard and understood. Give individuals who make suggestions the privilege to critique their own ideas before anyone else. When self-critique precedes collective critique, most negative points are volunteered by the people who brought up the idea in the first place. They tend to be much tougher on themselves than when the negative point is expressed by others.

When critiquing the contribution of others, point out the positive side first. Try not to formulate objections or discuss risks without suggesting solutions or offering strategies to manage such risks. The objective is to keep the original contribution and possibly to improve on it rather than systematically focusing on its negative aspects. The idea will ultimately be discarded if its implementation and salvage costs outweigh its benefits.

This protocol saves time and reduces defensive behavior. It yields more synergy than classical brainstorming techniques.

85. Inspire goodwill.

Compromise on minor points. Keep the greater good always in mind. Tap the strength that comes from mutual trust and support. Show *esprit de corps.* Practice humility, particularly when facing potential conflicts even if your ego takes a beating.

86. Refrain from responding to personal attacks.

Try to ignore them if you can. Responding to aggression in-kind is counterproductive. It escalates dysfunctional conflicts. Moreover, it leads to sidetracking. Success is a fleeting hope for the quick-tempered.

87. Record decisions.

Assign responsibility and a timeframe for following up each decision. Inform those who ought to know about the meeting's conclusions.

The practice of recording decisions as they are reached and immediately allocating responsibility and a timeframe for each decision to be carried out has proven effective ever since Admiral Rickover introduced the concept to the U.S. Navy in the seventies. The *Harvard Meeting Form*[2] translates the Rickover concept into a practical instrument to speed up meeting planning, management and follow-up.

88. Show appreciation and celebrate.

Thank those who made a contribution to the meeting or helped you in any way, particularly those who are candid and considerate. But don't overdo it. You can hurt people with undeserved or excessive compliments, particularly when they believe you are insincere.

Think of a token present to show your appreciation to the support staff and others. If your budget and time permit it, propose a toast. Celebrating even minor progress or achievements is a highly valued tradition in the Pacific Rim and in several European countries. If you are the subject of praise, handle it honestly.

References and notes

1.   James L. Heskett, W. Earl Sasser, Jr. and Leonard A.
     Schlesinger, *Achieving Breakthrough Service for the
     Frontline Manager,* Facilitator's Guide, Harvard
     Business School Video Series, Boston.

2.   The *Meeting & Communication Form* is designed to
     help you implement the concepts advocated and
     practiced by Admiral Rickover. It is available from The
     Harvard Planner Group Tel: (819) 772-7777.

Personal notes

Section 10

Travel carefree

89. Assess the cost/benefits of travel.

Consider options such as teleconferencing, hosting the meeting in your city, delegating someone else, meeting halfway or combining multiple trips. Also consider meeting at a symposium or a periodic event of mutual interest. Sometimes, it is better to postpone a trip in order to meet more clients and generate more business. [1]

90. Save money and time on personal and business trips.

Retain the services of an experienced travel agent who values your time and works to save you money but not at the expense of convenience. Airline hubs, connections and rules, as well as hotel and car rental policies, are mind boggling. Leave it to an agent who strives to meet and exceed your needs.

I have retained the same travel agent for nearly twenty years even though she changed jobs three times. She does her utmost to get me a seat with the most leg room on airlines with the highest punctuality and safety ratings. She avoids booking on the last daily flight, keeping it as a contingency in case of a delay or a cancellation. She tries to minimize the number of connections, particularly via airports known for delays. My clients and I save several thousands of dollars each year thanks to her know-how and business acumen. And I also save time by not having to spell out my idiosyncratic needs and billing requirements for each trip.

If feasible, reserve your airline ticket early and pre-select your seats and special meals. Request a free home or office delivery of your boarding pass in advance. Reconfirm 72 hours before your return flight. It is a "must" on international routes. I also make a point of systematically calling the airline prior to leaving for the airport to make sure the flight is neither delayed nor cancelled.

You can keep your flying cost down by traveling off-times with most airlines. Consider leaving Saturdays instead of Sundays especially if your destination is worth it. The savings on airfare may exceed the cost of your room and board for the extra hotel night.

If you are making two trips to the same city (even for a day but not during the same week), you can still take advantage of the Saturday night discount while remaining at home during the week-end. Ask your travel agent to issue two tickets. The first one should cover your first departure date combined with your last return date. The second ticket should be used to return from your first trip (first voucher) and to start your second trip (second voucher). This is legal and appropriate. Furthermore, the second ticket is frequently taxfree if your destination is out of the country.

Students and anyone with a flexible travel schedule can save up to 60% on flight and hotel room costs through last-minute travel clubs. Make sure you understand the restrictions associated with this option, which should not be used for business travel or other trips with inelastic schedules.

Join the American Automobile Association (AAA), The Canadian Automobile Association (CAA) or their foreign counterpart. It's worth it even if you don't own a car. Your membership entitles you to substantial savings with selected car rental agencies, hotels and restaurants. The AAA rates may sometimes be better than corporate, military or government rates. I always call to check it out in advance. In addition, you get traveler's checks without any service charge, free protection against lost or stolen credit cards, free accident insurance, 24-hour emergency road service, and free towing. A personal trip counselling service includes detailed itinerary tips; free state and regional maps; camp and tour books listing tourist attractions, restaurants and approved hotels/motels. As a member, you can also call the AAA or CAA Facts Division toll-free for information on all aspects of motoring from traffic laws to car purchase and maintenance.

The Platinum and the Lifetime Membership cards of American Express, Diners/En Route gold cards, some MasterCard and Visa gold or affinity cards, as well as your professional association memberships, provide you with special travel benefits including life and casualty insurance. Join your airline lounge club to check-in faster. You can also avoid lining up for your car if you reserve it with a club or a VIP card from

a major car rental company. If you plan to travel
frequently, invest a few minutes to find out the
privileges and features of each card that are pertinent
to you. Don't rely on your memory; record them in
your Harvard Planner®. Last but not least, you can
negotiate hotel rates by calling the hotel directly instead
of dialing their general 800 toll-free line. By doing the
same thing with the local car rental desk, you may get
a free upgrade.

Try to use public phones with your calling card and
save on hotel charges especially when waiting for someone or for a flight. For less than two dollars, you can
send a message via *Message Mail* when you can't get
through. Your respondent will be called every 5 to 15
minutes until your message is received.

Some telephone companies charge excessive rates for
long distance calls, particularly overseas. When in
doubt, ask for a rate quote via 0 or 00.

Should you plan to transmit data or faxes using your
laptop, verify with the hotel in advance to ensure that
it can be done from your room rather than from the
business centre where you would pay a premium. I had
the misfortune of staying in a hotel where the telephone
plugs were made incompatible with those of regular
modems to make the customer pay extra.

91. Travel light.

Save time with carry-on luggage only. Thus, you avoid
loss, damage and theft, three growing predicaments
facing most international airlines. Furthermore, you

gain 10 to 15 minutes on each trip and much more on international flights. If you must check luggage, add your detailed flight itinerary with dates and hotel information to your name and address card. Never check your prescription drugs, your Harvard Planner® or whatever clothes or documents you will require during the first 48 hours of your trip.

You run the risk of venous stasis, pulmonary emboli and blood clot if you frequently take trips lasting over two hours. One aspirin daily, upon medical advice, and brisk walks before the flight can reduce the chance of blood clot formation. Avoid dehydration by drinking water or fruit juice every hour and by not taking alcohol, tea, coffee or carbonated soft drinks. Stretch and, as Dr. Forgey suggests, "walk up and down the aisle every 30 minutes, loosen and tighten abdominal and gluteal muscles periodically. Take occasional slow, deep breaths. Various isometric exercises help prevent cramping and travel fatigue as well as enhance blood flow."[2]

During the flight, "wear loose clothing and shoes. Use layers of clothing so that you can adjust to changes in cabin temperature."[3] Avoid clothes made of leather or synthetics. Use fire-retardant clothing made of cotton or wool. In case of emergency, they can also be used as a mask against smoke inhalation – a major cause of death in air accidents.

Buy a durable suitcase with sturdy, water-resistant materials and pockets to protect fragile or bulky items. The Samsonite Ultralight® weighs less than five pounds and features special wheels and ballistic resistant material that resists being torn or punctured. If your suit-case does not have wheels, a small heavy-duty luggage carrier can help prevent spinal injury and back pains. To make sure you don't lose it in the overhead compartments, as a surprising number of passengers do, attach your business card to it. I set my watch to ring at the time of arrival to be sure I don't forget anything in the plane.

Always keep your suitcase ready to avoid last minute rushing. Keep in it a duplicate set of your toiletries, vitamins and cosmetics, underwear, contact lenses or eyeglasses, shoes and articles for fitness or jogging, a travel-size hair dryer with built-in plugs for North American and European outlets and a small and reliable wake-up clock. General Electric has a variety of hair dryers that are robust, safe, reliable, long lasting and affordable. For the clock, consider the credit-card sized calculator from Seiko. It includes, at your fingertips, a currency rate exchanger and time display for major world cities.

Put spillage-prone supplies into individual zip-lock plastic bags and place them securely in your toiletry case or pouch. Upon your return, replace personal care supplies when you unpack. Don't wait until the eve of the next trip.

Try to complete your clothing selection for each trip at least one day before departure. Consider cotton and wool articles that don't wrinkle and ties and shirts that match all suits and formal wear.

92. Plan a safe and comfortable trip.

If you plan to go out of the country, ask the *International*

Travel Advisory Service of your government for current information regarding the safety and security of the places where you intend to stay. For each foreign trip, I call the Department of State, Washington (D.C.) hotline at (202) 647-5225 to inquire into the latest security threats, local crime and violence conditions, political unrest, food and health risks, driving and weather hazards, customs and currency restrictions, and other traveling tips pertinent to my destination.

I call twice for each foreign trip; first immediately on assignment and second 48 hours before departure. With the first call, I assess the cost/benefits of going. Recently, I rescheduled a business trip three times to a major country where a failed coup led to frequent student demonstrations and random acts of piracy in the coastal areas where my client was located. I refused two invitations to speak about strategy and international project management in another country. I also declined to fly with an airline that had defective maintenance procedures, thanks to a warning from the State Department hotline. The second call is to obtain an update, particularly on poor social climate or weather conditions.

I also consult William W. Forgey's *Travelers' Medical Resource - A guide to Health & Safety Worldwide.*[4] This affordable book describes both the endemic and occasional risks that you should know before departing anywhere. It also offers detailed descriptions of local diseases and tips about prevention, immunization and treatment. It has chapters on useful addresses including U.S. and Canadian embassies, on travel insurance, and even on motion sickness and jet lag prevention.

I particularly like the *Herchmer Individual Country Database.* Updated on a weekly basis, this computerized service integrates data available from reliable sources including the Atlanta Center for Disease Control (CDC) and The World Health Organization (WHO) in Geneva.[5]

Order enough local currency and travelers cheques for the entire trip from your bank or credit union several days in advance. Some financial institutions such as BancAmerica will deliver international money orders and a small amount of foreign currency to your office at no extra cost. Try to use your credit cards wherever you can. It is safer and you usually fare better on exchange rates.

93. Avoid overnight transatlantic flights.

Major airlines now offer daylight service from North America to Europe particularly on Sundays. You arrive Sunday evening and you adjust faster to time zone changes, especially when you have a full business schedule the following days. Also, avoid overnight flights and *red-eye specials* across Canada and the USA. Even if you manage to take a nap, you pay a high price in de-stabilizing your metabolism.

94. Beware of the trap of the new taxicab driver.

Know precisely where you are going in town. If you are not sure about the distance and directions, ask the car rental agents before leaving the airport. They know their town. I have found them eager to help.

95. Save time on travel reports.

When you check in, ask your hotel clerk to set up your account with separate bills for personal and business expenses to speed up your travel claim. I use a different credit card for each.

96. Sleep well.

Prudent time managers try not to skip a good night's sleep. Request a quiet room away from elevators, partying floors, discotheques and conventioneers. If the room is not soundproof, bring a sound conditioner or earplugs to help you sleep. During the winter, request a clean humidifier when the air is too dry.

97. Don't give up exercise.

Stay at the right place. More and more hotels such as the Embassy Suites in Washington D.C. provide a treadmill or a stationary bike in the room. If you can't bike or run, consider swimming or stair-climbing.

98. Plan your meals.

Plan meals ahead of time in hotels where Room Service permits it. Eat in moderation. Consult your physician about taking unflavored sugar-free fibre such as *Novomucilax*[6] along with a good supply of vitamins (C, B50, E, and one-a-day multi-vitamins/multi-mineral formula, Spirulina pure microalgae capsules) to make up for the deficiencies of business meals when traveling. Even under the most stringent time constraints, do not skip a meal.

99. Manage your wake-up time.

Do not rely on hotel operators alone for wake-up calls; set your watch or clock as a contingency. Make sure the wake-up time is a.m. not p.m. particularly if the display uses the 12-hour standard. Europeans visiting North America are often trapped. They inadvertently set their room alarm to 7 p.m. instead of 7 a.m.

References and notes

1. Alec Mackenzie, *The Time Trap,* Amacom, American Management Association, 1991 revised edition, ISBN 0-8144-7760-7, $12.95.

2. William W. Forgey, M.D., *Travelers' Medical Resource – A Guide to Health & Safety Worldwide,* ICS Books, Inc., Merrillsville, Indiana, 1993, ISBN 0-934-802-62-9, $19.95.

3. See Reference 2 above.

4. See Reference 2 above.

5. You can reach the Herchmer Medical Consultants by dialing their toll free number at 1-800-336-8334 or (219) 769-0866. You can also send a FAX to (219) 769-6035.

6. *Novomucilax* is available in pharmacies. For a one-year supply, write to G. Lalonde, Pharmacist, 381 Maloney Blvd., Gatineau, Canada J8P 1E3.

Personal notes

Section 11

Stretch your body and soul

100. Prevent stress risks and burnouts.

"The greatest toll from stress may come not from a divorce, the loss of a job, and other major traumatic changes or misfortunes, but from the minor yet frequent annoyances we experience daily -- getting stuck in traffic, gaining a few pounds, having an argument at work . . . . Relatively unimportant hassles often have a greater effect on health -- increasing risk of high blood pressure, asthma attacks, and possibly even chest pains -- than do larger-scale traumas in life. Such were the findings of a study conducted by Richard Lazarus and colleagues at the University of California at Berkeley. . . . What is fascinating and encouraging about these findings is that they suggest that although hassles and stress are unavoidable parts of daily life, we *can* do something about them and the adverse effects they have on health."[1]

Stress and burnouts squander energy and affect judgement. Dr. Herbert Benson of The Harvard Medical School suggests a proven and relatively simple approach to managing stress – the ten-minute *Relaxation Response*. Try it. Users have experienced real improvement in personal health, productivity, and mental performance, as well as lower blood pressure. Do it once or twice a day at least two hours after a meal. Sit quietly in a comfortable position and close your eyes. "Relax all your muscles slowly and deeply starting from your feet and up to your face. Breathe easily and naturally through your nose for about 10 minutes. As you breathe out, say the word *one* to yourself. You may open your eyes to check the time, but do not use an alarm. When you finish, sit quietly for several minutes, first with your eyes closed and then later with your eyes opened. Maintain a passive attitude. Relaxation will come with practice. Try to ignore distracting thoughts by repeating *one*."[2]

101. Remain alert.

Avoid exhaustion. Don't let the pressure build up beyond a reasonable level of discomfort.

Break your moment of tension. Take a short walk outside the office. Make a quick call to a friend or a family member. Stretch or meditate even for a couple of minutes. Take a short nap in a quiet area to increase your productivity and your energy level. Make up for the time, if company policy requires you to. Your mind and body will certainly appreciate the break.

102. Curtail night-shift work and driving.

"One out of every six American workers is involved in shift work, and industry analysts are beginning to assess its effects on the desynchronization of biological clocks. Shift workers' susceptibility to peptic ulcers and other stomach disorders is two to three times greater than the general population's. Their productivity is also significantly lower. According to a spate of studies, worker error peaks between 3:00 a.m. and 5:00 a.m. A study done on the trucking industry found that the chance of an accident increases by 200 percent at 5:00 a.m."[3]

The facts support the need for extreme caution in undertaking risk-prone activities at night. At least consult your physician before accepting regular night-shift work. If feasible, try to save lives by staying off intercity roads at night.

103. Watch your diet and liquor consumption.

Eat moderately. Do not skip breakfast, or your performance will ultimately suffer. Keep your diet balanced in fibre, proteins, vitamins and carbohydrates. There is no better choice than raw vegetables, whole grain bread, pasta, yogurt, cheese, milk, fresh fruits, unsweetened juices and, occasionally, lean meat.

Keep hydrated with no less than seven glasses of fresh water per day. Do not indulge in meals and snacks with high fat, sugar, salt or cholesterol content. Food such as bacon, fried or canned food, potato chips, regular ice cream, chocolate bars or buttered popcorn should be avoided.

Avoid alcohol during lunch. It affects your creativity and effectiveness at work. If you can, stay away from drinking altogether except on rare social occasions. Excessive drinking and unhealthy food contribute to obesity, diabetes, liver disease, coronary problems, breast cancer and even premature death.[4]

104. Recharge your batteries.

Respect your biological clock.[5] Sleep at least seven hours per day in a well-ventilated dust-free room. According to current sleep research, the benefits are unequivocal. The evidence shows that sleep deprivation contributes to stress and other health problems.[6] Don't sleep late. If you are tired, sleep extra hours once a week to catch up. Do not carry your sleep deficit beyond a week. It will affect your performance, your memory, your safety on the road, your health and your mental and emotional balance.

If you wake up in the night because of noises from traffic, neighbors or a snoring roommate, consider a sound conditioner or earplugs to reduce the disturbance. You will fall asleep faster and awaken more relaxed. Hassle-free sleep is crucial for high-performers. You can also use your conditioner if you take a brief nap during your lunch time. It masks typing and light manufacturing noises.[7]

105. Prevent sleeping disorders.

According to CBC Prime Time News, one out of three North Americans suffer from sleeping disorders[8]; there are endless known causes for this predicament. Even poor posture at work and high-heeled shoes can cause back pain and make it difficult for you to sleep. Your mattress should be firm, but not stiff. Your sleeping position should not alter the spine's natural curves. Use pillows if you sleep on your stomach or on your side with knees bent.

If you start losing sleep over issues or problems facing you or others, take it as an early warning signal to act promptly on the cause of the insomnia. Don't hesitate to call on your physician, counselor or banker. In the meantime, keep your diet balanced and don't compromise your fitness needs.

106. Treasure and protect your moments of solitude.

Find the opportunity to truly avail yourself of moments of complete solitude. Go winter camping, windsurfing or solo-hiking for a day or two. I take a short walk alone or retire in a quiet area at least once a week. "... being alone means togetherness—the recoming-together of me and nature, of me and being; the reuniting of me with all. For me, solitude especially means putting the parts of me back together—the unifying of myself whereby I can see once again that the little things are little and the big things are big. I believe that solitude is a profound and needed act of self-love and self-appreciation."[9]

107. Exercise.

Take care of the three basic needs of physical fitness, namely cardio-respiratory needs, stretching and strength.

Cardiovascular fitness requires twenty-five minutes of your time four days a week. You can build it by swimming, jogging, bicycling, hiking, brisk walking, stair-climbing or cross-country skiing. Besides burning extra calories and stabilizing your weight, cardiovascular fitness gives you endurance, vitality and energy in daily living. It is critical in the prevention of coronary heart disease and in managing stress. Work within your limits at a pace that is vigorous but not straining. The acid test is to be able to speak without losing your breath.

Stretching builds the necessary flexibility for running, skiing, swimming, cycling and other strenuous activities. It enhances circulation, posture and body movement. With it, you can alleviate low back pain or soreness in tendons and muscles. You develop flexibility by stretching for about fifteen minutes a day.

As Aaron Mattes observes in his excellent book *Flexibility – Active and Assisted Stretching,* ". . . even animals are often seen stretching before movement. Flexibility is an important adjunct to regain or maintain optimum health. Preventing postural problems and joint injuries should be a major goal for everyone. Physical and mental health may be improved with a carefully constructed program of mild stretching exercises, helping retain the quality of life that is reduced through loss of tissue elasticity and joint range." [10]

The book titled *Stretching* by Bob Anderson is another practical guide to stretching for beginners and professionals in competitive sports. It also contains useful hints about cardiovascular fitness, injury prevention and nutritious eating. [11]

Current medical research indicates that "stretching cold muscles, especially on a cold day, can lead to injuries . . . . The best way to prepare for jogging, bicycling, squash, or any other exercise is to warm up the muscles gently, and after that do your stretches." [12]

Strength, the last component of physical fitness, reduces the strain of daily activities and enhances performance in sports. It also reduces the risk of bone fatigue and degeneration (osteoporosis). You can achieve added strength by calisthenics and weight lifting three times a week.

Exercise steadily. Get it out of your way as early as possible, especially if you exercise outdoors. You will reduce your dependence on the afternoon weather and avoid the frustration and guilt associated with unfulfilled obligations. If you can't find the time for a complete work-out, at least take care of your cardiovascular system to avoid premature bypass surgery or a pacemaker.

If pressed for time, bike or run on a treadmill while watching the news or learning a skill on video. The Harvard Business School has an excellent executive training program on video. [13] Try it. If you are out of town, don't give up exercising.

Do not embark on a regular cardiovascular fitness or weight-lifting program without consulting your physician or your local sports medicine clinic. A treadmill stress test should be an essential part of your annual check-up. The clinic's staff should normally help you select a program that takes into account your objectives, availability and preferences, and is within your physical and budgetary means.

With regular exercise, "small changes happen every-day. The changes may be so slight that you don't really notice them in any one day. It is this accumulation of small, slight changes on a regular basis that leads to natural results. So, if you want to change, do it by being regular with rhythmical activity, stretching, and light, nutritious eating." [14] You will feel better and perform your favorite tasks with greater ease and *without torturing yourself.*

108. Reward yourself.

Consider regular massage therapy. "Massage alleviates, or at least decreases, pain and helps to relax muscle spasm. This increases blood circulation which, in turn, helps the body get rid of waste products, some of which produce pain. As well, recent studies have shown that being touched reduces both pain and anxiety." [15]

An experienced and certified health care professional can provide you with a sport or a Swedish massage to help you relax and bridge the gap between your body and soul. It is best to get a massage before retiring or when you can take a complete rest for at least a half hour afterwards.

References and notes

1. Notes from the Wellness Letter, University of California, Berkeley, CA, Tel: (510) 643-8016.

2. This text is a summarized version of the excellent and highly recommended paper written by Herbert Benson, *Time out from Tension,* Harvard Business Review Jan.- Feb. 1978.

   You can also acquire the 60-minute video cassette *The Relaxation Route: Is Stress a Problem to Your Life?* conducted by Eli Bay and produced by Soma Film & Video in 1991 for public TV broadcasters across Canada. The video comprises six exercises to practice and control stress. Contact Soma Film in Toronto, Canada at (416) 466-0822.

3. Jeremy Rifkin: *Time Wars: The Primary Conflict in Human History,* Henry Holt and Company, New York, ISBN 0-8050-0377-0, $24.00.

   In praising this outstanding book, Ralph Nader said: *"Time Wars* is a book you will read in a few hours but will reflect on for a lifetime . . . Jeremy Rifkin gets you thinking, as you never have before, about the consequences of different time concepts that prevail between cultures and between generations.''

4. In an extensive medical and lifestyle study involving 7,000 respondents for 25 years, Dr. Lester Breslow of the School of Public Health, University of California, Los Angeles; and Dr. Norman Breslow of the University of Washington, Seattle; discovered that an unhealthy lifestyle increased the risk of premature death and serious disablities. They learned that alcohol, smoking, inadequate physical activity, obesity, skipping a high protein and fibre breakfast and eating snacks with high sugar, fat or salt content reduce longevity.

5. Lester R. Bittel, *Right on Time, the Complete Guide to Time-Pressured Managers,* McGraw-Hill Inc., New York, p.16, ISBN 0-07-005585-8, $14.95.

6. In the study referenced in 4 above, Dr. Lester Breslow and Dr. Norman Breslow discovered that sleeping less than seven hours a night was among the culprits that added to the risk of premature death and serious disabilities.

7. For more information on sound conditioners, call Comtrad's toll-free number 1-800-992-2966.

8. Canadian Broadcasting Corporation, *Special Report on Sleeping Disorders*, CBC Prime Time News, Toronto, April 1994.

9. Hugh Prather, *Notes to Myself, My Struggle to Become a Person,* Bantam Books, New York, ISBN 0-553-08629-4, 1976.

10. Aaron Mattes, *Flexibility – Active and Assisted Stretching,* Aaron Mattes Publishers, 2932 Lexington Street, Sarasota, Florida 34231-6118.

11. Notes from the Wellness Letter, University of California, Berkeley, CA, Tel.: (510) 643-8016.

12. Bob Anderson, *Stretching for Everyday Fitness and for Running, Tennis, Racquetball, Cycling, Swimming, Golf and other Sports,* Shelter Publications, P.O. Box 279, Bolinas, CA 94924, ISBN 0-936070-01-3 also published by Random House, ISBN 0-394-73874-8.

13. The Harvard University Video Series comprises some of the best films on decision-making, including *Total Quality, Competitive Strategy, Information Technology* and *Achieving Breakthrough Service for the Frontline Manager;* available from HBS Video Series, Soldiers' Field, Boston.

14. Bob Anderson, *Stretching;* see reference 12 above.

15. Excerpts are from the booklet titled *Back Basics* about the nature of back pain and ways to relieve it; published by the Back Association of Canada, 83 Cottingham Street, Toronto, Ontario, M4V 1B9.

Personal notes

_____

_____

_____

_____

_____

_____

_____

_____

_____

_____

_____

_____

_____

_____

_____

_____

_____

_____

_____

_____

Section 12

Make life worth living

109. Cherish genuine friendships.

With a new acquaintance, we tend to notice each other's virtues; then we see each other's flaws. "If we make it through this latter stage then maybe we will see each other and truly be friends."[1]

Cherish, respect, protect and help your friends. Start with your parents, spouse and family. Support their struggle for high ideals. Don't take their friendship or love for granted. Listen to them and pay attention to their feelings. Discuss your relationship openly and honestly at least twice a year. Nurture it constantly and forever.

When a friend is involved in a conflict with someone, exercise caution in your behavior but don't be a fence-sitter. Validate perceptions. Help resolve the issue quietly and discreetly. De-escalate tempers. Avoid taking sides at the expense of ethics. Be vigilant about fairness and privacy.

110. Socialize tactfully.

Invite only one or two people to meet with you at a time. Devote your full attention to one person, instead of responding superficially to many. Whether it is during lunchtime or after hours, socializing is not wasted time if the focus is on learning rather than gossiping. It is an effective way to grow, to learn about yourself or others and to be accessible to them. Regard it as part of the job.

111. Build allies.

Cultivate trust. Use empathy. Avoid coercive power. Nurture respect. Go out of your way to help others while encouraging self-help. Educate your staff, suppliers, clients and customers to do the same. Promote effective time management for the common good.

112. Have fun.

Don't take yourself too seriously. Use decent, good and clean humour appreciated by your associates. Laugh and laugh at yourself when in good company. Avoid abusive cynicism and coercive humour that is disguised defamation with racial, ethnic or gender overtones. With respect to jokes, abstain when in doubt about their merit.

113. Don't poison your life.

Free yourself from envy, jealousy, greed, vindictiveness and aimless gossiping. Don't dwell on the past. You will accomplish more and grow faster without these poisonous deadweights.

114. Don't slip into codependency status.

You are codependent if your emotions, feelings, behavior and self-worth are severely handicapped by your obsessive determination to rescue a troubled friend, relative or colleague who is consistently oblivious to constructive dialogue and problem solving. If you are in this predicament, don't waste your time. Seek professional help for your troubled partner, avoid hostility and stop worrying about and controlling him or her. Take responsibility for your own well-being. Seek professional help if needed. Find your inner peace and make the most of your day.

As Melodie Beattie says: "Have a love affair with yourself . . . Out of high self-esteem will come true acts of kindness . . . not selfishness. The love we give and receive will be enhanced by the love we give ourselves."[2]

115. End dysfunctional relationships gracefully.

Terminate hostile and unproductive relationships promptly and gracefully. It will be tough. And, if you can't succeed on your own, consider the practical seminar of The Gestalt Institute of Cleveland: *Finishing and Letting Go.*[3] In the meantime, avoid abrasive language and empty rhetoric.

116. Stop reading and watching trivia.

Cut your TV viewing time to a minimum. You can exercise, meditate, learn or share the time you gain with people you value.

117. Concentrate on the vital few.

We are not concentrating on the vital few when we cease growing and waste our time on futile or marginal activities. When genuine joy in life is lacking, when the feelings, aspirations and needs we have repressed trip us because of neglect, we stagnate.

Use the opportunity cost of your time to respond to the twin pressures of work demands and personal equilibrium. Apply the Pareto rule of thumb: 20% of your activities account for 80% of the results. Examine your performance every day to highlight the specific actions that truly advance the fulfillment of your mission. Post major achievements on a personal board as a reinforcement.

118. Prune work backlog at least once a month.

Priorities are relative and dynamic. Re-evaluate objectives, values and relationships. Cut out nonessential work. Abort dysfunctional projects promptly and wisely.

119. Learn new skills to face greater challenges every day.

Being a lifetime learner expands your ability to take calculated risks and confront your fears. If you don't keep learning, you cease to grow.

Learning does not guarantee immediate success. So don't be discouraged if you fail. Einstein thought ninety-nine times that the conclusion he had reached was false. "The hundredth time, I was right," he said.

The great French composer Jean-Philippe Rameau was a lifetime learner who began writing music at the age of fifty. He left us thirty pieces including *Les Boréades,* the most remarkable opera to be written after Mozart and Monteverdi. Rameau was eighty years old when he composed *Les Boréades.*

Promote lifetime learning in your family, your organization and community.[4] There is no better way to cultural, social and economic growth.

120. Take time off.

Nobel Prize Laureate Francis Crick says: "It is well-documented that the best way to have ideas is first of all to immerse yourself in a subject for longish periods – like months or more – in which you study intensely, and then step away and do something else – go on holidays, go out dancing, or something like that. Very often ideas come in this sort of incubation period."[5]

121. Break the *work-and-spend* vicious cycle.

"A final impediment to using leisure is the growing connection between free time and spending money . . . Vacations, hobbies, popular entertainment, eating out, and shopping itself are all costly forms of leisure."[6]

Select leisure activities that will bring joy, genuine satisfaction, compassion, kindness and inner peace without burdening your budget.

122. Be altruistic at least once a day.

Invest in the common good. Take time to serve society while you can. If you have pets, nurture them. They don't waste your time. "It is a known medical fact that people with pets live longer."[7]

Educate the youth and learn from them. Comfort those in need. Give blood. You will feel great and you will go a long way toward making the world a better place for you and for those you care most about.

123. Experience flow.

Such feelings – which include concentration, absorption, deep involvement, joy, a sense of accomplishment – are what people describe as the best moments in their lives. They can occur almost anywhere, at any time, provided one is using psychic energy in a harmonious pattern. It is typically present when one is singing or dancing, engaged in a religious ritual or in sports, when one is engrossed in reading a good book or watching a great performance. It is what the lover feels talking to her beloved, the sculptor chiseling marble, the scientist engrossed in her experiment. I have called these feelings flow experiences, because many respondents in our studies have said that during these memorable moments they were acting spontaneously, as if carried away by the tides of a current.[8]

In order to experience flow, you need clear goals, immediate and ongoing feedback, opportunities and skills. A sense of power to act decisively, a sense of urgency, a sense of being part of a greater entity, and total concentration on the task at hand contribute to this profound experience. The experience becomes rewarding and worth doing for its own sake.[9]

124. Record your achievements.

Don't rely on your memory. Remember Franklin's daily question: "What good have I done today?"[10] Post your performance every day in your Harvard Planner®. Well-documented facts will help you plan ahead and even get a raise and a promotion.

125. Seize the day, the moment.

> Let us make today a creative day; let us look to the day with objectives; let us regard the day as our opportunity. We must do everything we can to make each day a life in itself . . . One day at a time. You add up a succession of creative days—and you have a creative life . . . You will achieve this creative day if you can develop your emotional, spiritual and thinking qualities.[11]

There is tremendous room for personal and professional growth for people willing to work smarter and live better. Don't wait. Consider every day a window of opportunity to shape your future. Life is too short to bore yourself. Don't waste it. Take time to live life fully and enjoy it thoroughly. Why not start now?

References and notes

1. This paragraph on a new acquaintance is adapted from Hugh Prather, *Notes to Myself, My struggle to become a person,* Bantam Books, New York, ISBN 0-553-08629-4, 1976.

2. Melodie Beattie, *Codependent No More,* Hazelden Educational Materials, Center City, ISBN 0-89486-402-5.

3. Gestalt Institute of Cleveland, 1588 Hazel Drive, Cleveland, Ohio 44106-1791, Tel: (216) 421-0468.

4. Among the best books on building and sustaining a learning organization is:

    Richard Beckhard and Wendy Pritchard, *Changing the Essence, The Art of Creating and Leading Fundamental Change in Organizations,* Jossey-Bass Inc., 350 Sansome St., San Francisco, CA94104, ISBN 1-55542-412-0, available from PDI, Tel: (819) 772-7777.

5. B. Eugene Griessman, *The Achievement Factors: Candid Interviews with Some of the Most Successful People of Our Time,* Dodd, Mead & Co., New York, 1987, p.75, ISBN 0-396-08977-1, $18.95.

6. Juliet Schor, *The Overworked American,* Basic Books, Harper Collins, New York, 1991, ISBN 0-465-05434-X.

7. Milo O. Frank, *How to Run a Successful Meeting in Half the Time,* Pocket Books, Simon & Schuster, New York, ISBN 0-671-72601-3.

8. Mihaly Csikszentmihalyi, *The Evolving Self,* Harper Collins Publishers, 1993, p. 176, ISBN 0-06-016677-0.

9. Mihaly Csikszentmihalyi, *Flow: The Psychology of Optimal Experience, Steps Toward Enhancing The Quality of Life,* Harper Perennial, A Division of Harper Collins Publishers, 1990, ISBN 0-06-092043-2.

10. Benjamin Franklin, *The Autobiography and Other Writings,* Penguin Books, 1986, ISBN 0-14-039052-9.

11. Maxwell Maltz, *Creative Living for Today,* Pocket Books, Simon & Schuster, 1974, ISBN 0-671-78773-X.

Personal notes

30-day Action Plan

Review the personal notes you took at the end of each section and draft an action plan to improve your time management.

• *Personal time:*

_____

_____

_____

_____

_____

_____

_____

_____

_____

_____

_____

• *Team time:*

_____

_____

_____

_____

_____

_____

_____

_____

_____

_____

_____

• *Corporate performance:*

_____
_____
_____
_____
_____
_____
_____
_____
_____
_____
_____
_____
_____

• *Family time:*

_____
_____
_____
_____
_____
_____
_____
_____
_____
_____
_____
_____
_____
_____
_____

• *Performance of your allies (Clients, Suppliers, Shareholders, Governments, etc.):*

_____

_____

_____

_____

_____

_____

_____

_____

_____

_____

_____

• *Others:*

_____

_____

_____

_____

_____

_____

_____

_____

_____

_____

_____

Please record these actions in your Harvard Planner®.

Index

Abrahmson,
   Dr. Samuel 65, 67
*Achievement Factors:
   Candid Interviews
   with Some of the
   Most Successful
   People of Our
   Time, The* 32, 148
*Achieving Breakthrough
   Service for the
   Frontline
   Manager* 110
Active intervention 26
Adams, James L. 13
American Automobile
   Association (AAA)
   115
American Express
   Travelers'
   Division 65
Anderson, Bob 132, 137
Andrews, Kenneth 14
Anton, Charles 80
Assumptions, challenge
   of 5
*Autobiography and
   Other Writings,
   The* 149
Automation

routine tasks 87
computers 88

Back Basics xvii, 137
Badaracco,
   Joseph L.Jr. 14
Beattie,
   Melodie xvii, 143,
   148
Beckhard,
   Richard 19, 58
Bégin, Luc 15
Benson,
   Dr. Herb xvii, 127,
   135
Bergstrom, A. Blair xviii
Bittel, Lester R. 136
Bloom, Allan xviii, 25, 31
Booher, Dianna 89
Breslow,
   Dr. Norman 136
Breslow, Dr. Lester 136
*Briser la dictature du
   temps* 79
Burnout 127

Canadian Automobile
   Association
   (CAA) 115

Can Ethics Be Taught?
  Perspectives,
  Challenges, and
  Approaches at
  Harvard Business
  School 14
Car rental 116
Change, plan for 7
Changing the Essence,
  The Art of Creating
  and Leading Fun-
  damental Change in
  Organizations 148
Charan, Ram 70
Cleese, John 99
Closing of the American
  Mind, The xviii, 31
Codependency 143
Codependent No More xvii
Commuting 53
Competitive
  Advantage 59
Competitive Advantage
  of Nations, The 59
Competitive Strategy:
  Techniques for
  Analyzing
  Industries and
  Competitors 58
Computer software 88
Conceptual Block-
  busting: A Guide to
  Better Ideas 13
Consulting Skills 67

Corporate
  mission 24, 25,
  28-30
Corporate
  performance 37
Cox, Jeff 12
Creative Living for
  Today xviii, 149
Credit cards 115
Critical mass 25
Csikszentmihalyi,
  Mihaly xviii, 149
Cutting Paperwork in
  the Corporate
  Culture 89

de Bono,
  Edward xviii, 1, 9,
  12, 14
de Bono's Thinking
  Course xvi, 12
Deadlines 40-42
  fiscal 40
  official/
  ceremonial 40, 41
  operational or
  functional 40, 41
  overall
  completion 40, 41
Decision making 1, 2, 4
Decision-support
  systems 87
Delegation 63-69
  daily workload 64

apprenticeship 66
options 67
Deporter, Bobbi xv
Desjardins, Alphonse 3
Desk top publishing 87
Dictaphones 85
Diet 129
Do-lists 44
Documents,
    creation of 87
Dominant coalition 25
Drucker, Peter 35
Dysfunctional
    relationships 143

*Edward de Bono's
    Thinking Course* 14
Edwards,
    Paul 73, 79, 80
Edwards,
    Sarah 73, 79, 80
*Electronic Page
    Processing, Pre-
    Press Savings
    and Book
    Manufacturing* 89
Ellsworth, Richard 14
Ergonomics 73
*Essence of a Proactive
    Life, 2 Practical
    Essays on Life and
    Career Planning*
    20, 31
Ethics 10

*Ethics in Practice:
    Managing the
    Moral
    Corporation* 14
*Éthique à l'usage de
    mon fils* 15
Éthique et Ingénierie 15
Etica Para Amador 15
Evolving Self, The xviii, 149
Exercise 131-134

Factional Analysis 56
Fax trap 83
    use, of 116
Filing 83
*Finishing and
    Letting Go* 143
*Flexibility--Active and
    Assisted
    Stretching* xviii, 132,
    136
*Flow: The Psychology
    of Optimal
    Experience,
    Steps Toward
    Enhancing The
    Quality
    of Life* xviii, 146,
    149
Food and Agricultural
    Organization 2
Food assistance
    program 2
Forgey, Dr.

William W. 117, 123
Franklin, Benjamin 149
Friendship 141
Future Positive 14

GE Money Machine:
   How its Emphasis
   on Performance
   Built a Colossus of
   Finance 70
General Electric xviii, 64, 70
Gentile, Mary C. 14
Goal setting 19-23
Goldratt, Eliahu M 12.
Griessman,
      B. Eugene 32, 148
Grove, Andrew S. 58

Harvard Business
   School 69
Harvard Meeting
   Form 104, 109, 110
Harvard Planner® xi, 44,
   51, 78, 104, 116
Harvard® Time
   Log 6, 12, 95
Herchmer Individual
   Country Database
   120, 123
Hernacki, Mike xv
Heskett, James L. 110
High leverage
   activities 38
High-Output

Management: The
   President of
   Intel, one of the Na-
   tion's Premier High
   Technology Compa-
   nies, Shows How
   Managers Can In-
   crease Their Produc-
   tivity Dramatically 58
Hill, Norman 70
How to Get what You
   Want 13
How to Increase
   Employee Compe-
   tence 70
How to Organize Your
   Work and Your Life:
   Proven Time
   Management Tech-
   niques for Business
   Professionals and
   other Busy People 58
How to Prepare a Work
   Breakdown
   Structure 48
How to Run a
   Successful Meeting
   in Half the
   Time 149
How to Say 'No', Five
   Easy Ways 52, 58
Hull, Raymond 13

I am Right, You are

Wrong: From This to The New Renaissance; From Rock Logic to Water Logic 14
If you haven't the time to do it right, when will you find the time to do it over? 80
Information getting 4
International Development Agency 56
International Travel Advisory Service 118
Interview 104

Jarroson, Bruno 73, 79
Jones, Prof. Curtis H. 42, 47

Lakein, Alan 35
Lasting decisions 53
  correlation with workload 53-55
Lateral Thinking; Creativity Step by Step 14
Leadership and the Quest for Integrity 14
Legault, Georges A. 15
Levy, Larry 13
Life-building 141, 142

Mackenzie, Alec 35, 123
Mail trap 83

Maltz, Maxwell xviii, 149
Martin, Alain P. 12, 31, 32, 47, 59
Martin, James 99
Mattes, Aaron xviii, 132, 136
Mayer, Jeffrey 80
Meeting and Communication Form 110
Meetings 103-109, 113
  Audience 103
  Celebration of 109
  Compromise in 108
  Decisions, 108
  Direction of 107
  Frequency 103
  Issues, sequence of 107
  Location 105
  Planning 104
  Punctuality of 106
  Rehearsal for 106
  Scenarios 105
  Silence in 107
  Visuals for 105
Memory Jogger: A Pocket Guide of Tools for Continuous Improvement, The 47
Michael Porter on Competitive Strategy 59
Milo, Frank O. 149

Money Value of Time,
   The 47
Moskovitz,
   Robert 52, 58

Night-shift work 128
Notes to Myself, My
   Struggle to Become a
   Person xviii, 136, 148

Objective
   analysis 44
   setting 44
   validation 30
One-Minute What?
   The xv, xviii
Open door policy 52
Organization, desk 76
Organized To Be
   Best xix, 13, 75, 79,
   80
Overcommitments 52
Overworked American,
   The xviii, 148

Paperwork,
   reduction of 83
Pareto rule 144
Parks, Sharon Daloz 14
Pauling, Linus 30
Pepper, John 69
Phone Power 93, 99
Phone technology 93-96
   cellular phone 94

pager 95
smart phone 93
Piper, Thomas R. 14
Plastic words 85
Porter, Prof.
   Michael 56, 58, 69
Prather, Hugh xviii, 136,
   148
Pre-programmed
   decisions 55-57
Prime time 51, 95
Priority setting 4, 26,
   35-39
   classes of 36-39
   essential 37, 43
   futile 39
   important 37
   marginal or nice-to-
   have 38
   unavoidable obligation
   39
Pritchard, Wendy 148
Proactive
   intervention 27
Proactive Thinking
   Paradigm, The xv,
   12, 24, 30, 31, 32,
   35, 42, 47, 59
Productivity
   improvement 37
Programmed
   responses 86

Quantum Learning–

Unleashing the Genius in You xv
Questioning
 knowledge 4

Racine, Louis 15
Réflexions d'Alphonse Desjardins xviii, 12
Relaxation Response 127
Relaxation Route: Is Stress a Problem to Your Life?, The 135
Revenue-generating
 tasks 37
Reward, self 134
Rewards 68
Rifkin, Jeremy 79
Right on Time, the Complete Guide to Time-Pressured Managers 136
Risk Management 3, 27, 43

Sasser, W. Earl 110
Savater, Fernando 15
Schlesinger,
 Leonard A. 110
Schor, Juliet xviii
Security 77
Shepard, Herbert 19, 31
Shopping 76
Silver, Susan xix, 13, 75, 79, 80

Skill development
 stages 65, 66
Sleeping
 requirements 130
 disorders 130
socio-econographic
 profile 56
Solitude, need for 131
Solution
 implementation 3
Special Report on Sleeping Disorders 136
Speed, Simplicity and
 Self-Confidence 70
Spirulina pure micro-
 algae capsules 121
Stay-in-business work 37
Stay-out-of-trouble
 work 37
Strategic Risk Management 47
Strategy formulation 43
Stress
 management 127, 128
Stretching for Everyday Fitness and for Running, Tennis, Racquetball, Cycling, Swimming, Golf and other Sports 132, 137

Technology, use of 83, 85, 87, 88, 93-95
Technology Update 80

Telephone Behavior:
     The Power & The
     Perils 99
Telephone
     etiquette 94, 96, 97
     log 97
     public 116
Think Proactive 47
Thinking speed 1, 3
Tichy, Noel 70
Time, fill-in 45
     prime 51
     saving 74, 75, 86
     scheduling 44
     use of 5, 6, 42
     waste of 7-9, 51, 95
Time log 6
Time Out from
     Tension xvii, 135
Time Trap, The 123
Time Wars: The
     Primary Confict in
     Human History 79,
     135
Total Quality
     Management (TQM)
     6
Travel 113-122
     Agent 113, 114
     Airline 113, 114
     Costs 113, 114
     Credit card,
     use of 115
     Health during 117

Luggage 116
Traveler's Medical
     Resource--A guide to
     Health & Safety
     Worldwide 119, 123
Trouble with Dilemmas:
     Rethinking Applied
     Ethics, The 15
Type setting 87

Urgency 39-42

Value chain 9

Walther, George 93, 99
Warranties 75
Weiss, Brian 13
White, Jack E. 13
Whitebeck, Caroline 15
Wisdom 4
Work audit 5, 6
Work tracking 86
Work-and-spend
     cycle 145
Work-Out xviii, 64, 70
Working from Home:
     Everything You Need
     to Know about Living
     and Working Under
     the Same Roof 80
Working with Difficult
     People 9, 13
World Seminar: The
     Complete Project
     Management Cycle 12

About the Author

A. Paul Martin has trained over 30,000 decision-makers from leading companies in the U.S., Canada, Japan and Europe. His seminars and conferences on project management, strategy formulation, negotiation skills and the management of change have been attended by senior executives and managers from Alcan, Bell, Bechtel, Boeing, Esso, Fuji, General Electric, General Motors, IBM, Kawasaki, MetLife, Skanska, Spar Aerospace and the World Bank. In addition, Mr. Martin has provided training to a host of Government agencies and is a member of the non-partisan committee of executives advising the Prime Minister of Canada on government reform.

Mr. Martin is the inventor of the Harvard Planner®. He is also the creator of the Proactive Thinking Paradigm, an innovative framework with practical tools to facilitate mission setting, objective validation, strategy formulation, risk management, responsibility charting and implementation control in managing complex issues and tasks. In addition, Mr. Martin developed the Global Method, a project management technique used to manage capital and soft projects.

Information on seminars and workshops led by Mr. Martin may be obtained by calling (613) 730-7777 or by FAX at (613) 235-1115.

A new book from PDI!

ESSENCE OF A PROACTIVE LIFE

2 Practical Essays on Life & Career Planning
by Herbert Shepard

The first essay, *Life Planning,* helps readers build a life-worth-living and addresses such profound questions as "Who are we?" and "Who should we be?". It invites us to a candid self-examination which results in discovering those moments when we rejoice in life and find sources of fulfillment. The essay covers the three prerequisites for a deep gratification in life. When these prerequisites are in harmony we rejoice. *Life Planning* establishes a basis for living a meaningful life. It develops the awareness that we are responsible for the quality of our lives and that living fully means investing thoroughly in the creation of our experience. This investment involves risk and joy, two subjects thoroughly discussed in the last section of the essay.

How to Stay Alive, the second essay, is an invaluable guide for change agents. It offers eight principles based on the author's experience in working with decision-makers and change agents. These principles range from avoiding self-sacrifice to building experiments for success. Other topics explored include retaining optimism, capturing the moment and recommending the ingredients for successful innovation.

HERBERT SHEPARD was a pioneering figure in the Organization Development movement. He held faculty posts at several universities including M.I.T., where he received his doctorate in Industrial Economics; Case Western Reserve, where he founded and directed the first doctoral program in Organization Development; and Yale, where he developed a residency in administrative psychiatry. He has published widely and was President of The Gestalt Institute of Cleveland and of the Professional Development Institute from 1977 to 1985. In management consulting, Prof. Shepard's clients included Bell-Northern Research, Syncrude, TRW, Connecticut General Life Insurance Company, Union Carbide and many government departments in both the U.S.A. and Canada.

Invest one day in PDI's course

Flawless Time Management

and gain 30 days each year

Doing a superb job the first time is what this course is all about. *Flawless Time Management* helps you allocate your very limited time effectively in order to get the best out of your life. It provides proven tools and sound timesaving skills, most of which are not available elsewhere. The focus is on the *how-to's* of high performance in managerial, professional and administrative occupations.

This course yields no less than 30 working days per year in time savings or their equivalent in increased productivity for each participant. Equally applicable at home, the program offers new ways to accomplish highly valued family goals. It includes an intensive presentation on productivity using The Harvard Planner®.

Unlike many books and seminars on the topic of time management, this one-day program, its course materials and timesaving tools are truly unique. They are the product of twelve years of ongoing research conducted by A.P. Martin for PDI.

Investing just one day in PDI's *Flawless Time Management* will bring you the skills that are essential for lifelong learning and growth.

Flawless Time Management is practical in every sense of the word. There is no trivia. No time is wasted on futile exercises. You will have a full day devoted to the proven concepts and best practices that have been thoroughly tested to substantially increase your productivity and improve your quality of life. Guaranteed!

Please reserve your seat now at a location near you. Register by fax at (613) 235-1115 or call (613) 730-7777. If busy, dial (819) 772-7777.

Syd Bosloy

Syd Bosloy, Chairman
The Center for Excellence in Time Management

If you can't take "Flawless Time Management"
switch to The Harvard Planner®
and save 1.4 weeks each year

An affordable timesaver (price: $19 to $31), *The Harvard Planner®* outperforms Franklin Planner® and Day-Timer® in scheduling and space saving. A nationwide study by Ernst & Young indicated that customers who switch to *The Harvard Planner®* save 1.4 weeks a year (see below). With Harvard, you are not buying merely a scheduling tool, but you are opting for a proven system of lasting value backed by a long tradition of excellence and solid know-how.

ƎIJ ERNST & YOUNG   ▪ **Management Consultants**

March 31, 1993

Harvard Planner Assessment

Ernst & Young has conducted an independent market assessment of time management tools produced by The Professional Development Institute (PDI). The nationwide study involved participants from a number of large corporations including Systemhouse SHL, Bell, Motorola, the Royal Bank, and Ernst & Young.

The objective of the study was to determine specific time benefits, if any, realized by the participants as a result of using, for one month, the Harvard Planner. During the survey PDI agreed to maintain an arm's-length relationship with the participants. None of the participants were selected by PDI. All responses were returned directly to Ernst & Young.

The following findings are drawn from participants who have not taken the seminar offered by PDI.

All Participants Average:	14 minutes per day time saving
Manager level:	14 minutes per day time saving
Accountants:	15 minutes per day time saving
Others - including Support Staff:	13 minutes per day time saving

- On average, the above findings indicate that individuals using the Harvard Planner, will achieve savings of approximately 1.4 weeks per year (14 min. per day x 230 working days - holidays & sick leave excluded - = 1.43 wks per yr.). It is reasonable to assume that if such savings were consistently applied they may translate into a significant return on investment at the corporate level.

- Some three-quarters (74%) of the participants were using a different form of time planner when they began the survey.

- We have also received a range of positive feedback from the participants, who generally claim to be very pleased with the Harvard Planner and will continue to utilize this product in the future.

Tony P. Going
Principal

Feature	Journal Planners & Refills, Medium & Pocket, 1 page/day	Int'l., Original, Pocket size, Wire-O & Lexide cover or 6 holes	Int'l., Original, Desk & Medium size, Wire-O or 7 holes	Int'l., Original, Desk size, 3-hole punch, heavy paper	Ultralight, 2 pages/month, Pocket size, stitched	Professional Planner, Desk size, spiral Wire-O	Superplanner™, Desk/Med. size, Wire-O or 7 holes
Full-color *world atlas* from Oxford in the phone book	•	•			•	•	•
2-page *week-at-a-time*, weekdays highlighted in color	•	•			•	•	•
1 line/hour (4 fifteen-minute cells each), original model					•	•	•
2 lines/hour with 3 ten-minute cells each for appointments	•						
4 lines/hour for appointments each with fee column			•				•
1 page/day, 4 lines/hr. (3 five-minute cells)							•
1 cell/hour in a month-at-a-time format, 93 actions						•	
Action lines, each with a unique reference letter	•		•	•	•	•	•
One-month-at-a-time sheets with weekdays in color	•	•	•	•	•	•	•
Two-year-at-a-time in a handy foldout sheet, 2 colors	•	•		•	•	•	•
Delegation, rescheduling & deferring action features	•	•		•	•	•	•
Meeting & *communication* log (desk & medium sizes)	•	•		•	•	•	•
Project schedule & progress control forms in 2 colors	•	•		•	•	•	•
Goal-setting section: Annual and monthly sheets, 2 colors	•	•		•	•	•	•
Budgeting and financial control grid	•	•		•	•	•	•
5-year holiday section for US and Canadian holidays	•	•		•	•	•	•
Detailed list of holidays for over 120 countries	•	•		•	•	•	•
Telephone area codes (US, Canada & 120 countries)	•	•		•	•	•	•
Forms for notes, tabular reports, cheques and expenses	•	•		•	•	•	•
English only (E) or bilingual in English and French (B)	E	B	B	B	B	B	B

Harvard Planners®

Contents
Key Features

For your Harvard Planner®, mail, phone or fax your order to:

The Harvard Planner Group

70 Technology Boulevard, Hull, Canada J8Z 3H8

Please use our 24-hour FAX: (613) 235-1115

Order Desk: ☎ (613) 730-7777 or (819) 772-7777

Important: Clients outside Canada must use a credit card or a money order in US$.

- Planners are available seven months prior to the applicable calendar year.
- All orders must be prepaid. Prices subject to change without prior notice.
- Please send a cheque or use a credit card (Amex, Visa, MasterCard)

Please detail your mailing address and include the following in your order: credit card number and expiry date, surname, first name, title and company name (if applicable), complete mailing address with street name and number, room number, city, state/prov., zip/postal code, country, and phone and fax numbers.

To receive a complimentary catalogue on the complete range of management and support staff training, books and time management products, please contact us.

Price List (U.S.$)
Harvard Planners®

Item	Desk size 21×28 cm, 8.5×11" Code Quantity × Price		Medium size 14×21 cm, 5.5×8.5" Code Quantity × Price		Pocket size 9×16cm, 3.75×6.5" Code Quantity × Price	
Journal: 1 page/day, 4 lines/hour, 7-hole refills			2WR	× $29		
Harvard Superplanners: 2 pages/week						
Wire-O binding, regular paper	1S	× $27	2S	× $23		
7-hole refills, regular paper	1SR	× $27	2SR	× $23		
International Planners: 2 pages/week						
Wire-O binding, original, regular paper	1H	× $27	2H	× $23	3H	× $19
7-hole refills, original, regular paper	1HR	× $27	2HR	× $23	3HR	× $19
3-hole refills, original, heavy paper	1HX	× $31				
Add Leather Covers (price excl. planners)						
for any Wire-O bound Planner	4C	× $65	5C	× $57	6C	× $46
Add Leather Portfolios (price excl. refills)						
7-ring, zippered, (pocket: 6 rings, Velcro®)	4PR	× $89	5PR	× $76	6PR	× $63
3-ring, zippered for 3-hole refills, heavy paper	4PX	× $89				
Add Vinyl Binders (price excl. refills)						
7-ring binders for 7-hole refills	1VR	× $24	2VR	× $17		
Work Planning & Time Management Forms						
Action forms, 7-day do-list, 44 lines (desk: 150; med. & pocket: 200/set)	12A	× $10	12B	× $ 9	12E	× $ 9
Meeting Planning & Decision forms (desk: 150; med.: 200/set)	14A	× $10	14B	× $ 9	14E	× $ 9
Communication & Contact forms (desk: 150; med.: 200/set)	18A	× $10	18B	× $ 9	18E	× $ 9
Note & Tabular Report forms (desk: 150; med. & pocket: 200/set)	22A	× $10	22B	× $ 9	22E	× $ 9
Expense forms: business/personal (desk: 150; med. & pocket: 200/set)	30A	× $10	30B	× $ 9	30E	× $ 9
Cheque listing sheets (desk: 150; med. & pocket: 200/set)	31A	× $10	31B	× $ 9	31E	× $ 9
Harvard time logs, one set will serve 5 people (100/set)	35A	× $10				
Project Charter & Risk Analysis forms (desk: 150; med.: 200/set)	45A	× $10	45B	× $ 9		
Project Schedule & Cost Control sheets (desk: 100; med.: 200/set)	47A	× $10	47B	× $ 9	47E	× $ 9
Strategy Grids & Transition Risk forms (desk: 150; med.: 200/set)	55A	× $10	55B	× $ 9		
Responsibility/Accountability Charts (desk: 150; med.: 200/set)	60A	× $10	60B	× $ 9		
7-hole punch (6 holes for pocket size)	711	× $29	712	× $26	713	× $23
Book: **Essence of a Proactive Life**	V25	× $6				
Book: **Think Proactive**	V20	× $24				
Paper: **Work Breakdown Structure**	V8	× $12				
Book: **Bringing Time to Life**	V27	× $19				
Time Management Questionnaire (2 sets)	V29	× $12				
NASA space pens, slim, triple duration cartridge	PEN	× $22				

- **Add shipping & handling:** Canada & U.S.A.: **$6** for the first unit, plus **$2** for each additional unit
- Other countries: insured airmail **$15** for the first unit, plus **$9** for each additional unit
- **Residents of Canada only:** Add 7% GST to taxable total or include your exemption certificate (Our No. R104317938); **Ontario & Québec residents:** Add PST or QST
- Please note that above prices are in U.S.$.

Help your family and staff manage their time

A comprehensive Time Management Questionnaire has been designed by the author to help you and your allies assess your proficiency and needs in time management. The questionnaire provides respondents with a means to evaluate their understanding of time management, define its pertinence to their job and other aspects of their life and assess their training and coaching needs. Respondents can use the questionnaire to periodically track improvements in their skills and performance and to clarify their career and training objectives with their superiors at work during annual reviews.

A quick scoring system helps the respondents assess the risk of inadequate performance in their job and day-to-day life.

To order your questionnaire, fax PDI at (613) 235-1115 indicating your name, title, company, branch and complete street address for UPS delivery, telephone and fax number, credit card (Amex, Visa or Mastercard), card number and expiry date. Indicate the number of sets that you need. Each set costs U.S.$12. It contains 2 questionnaire booklets and is good for 2 respondents. Minimum order: one set, plus shipping and handling U.S.$6. Residents of Canada: add GST, plus PST if you live in Ontario or Québec. For corporate orders: send your cheque to PDI, 79 Fentiman Ave., Ottawa, ON K1S 0T7 Canada. All orders must be prepaid.